THAT DOESN'T MEAN
WHAT YOU THINK IT MEANS

THAT DOESN'T MEAN
WHAT YOU THINK IT MEANS

(
THE 150 MOST COMMONLY
MISUSED WORDS AND THEIR
TANGLED HISTORIES
)

ROSS PETRAS AND KATHRYN PETRAS

TEN SPEED PRESS
California | New York

CONTENTS

ACKNOWLEDGMENTS

Thanks as always to our extraordinary editor Lisa Westmoreland (TG!), amazing agent Andrea Somberg, dauntless designer Chloe Rawlins, peerless production manager Dan Myers, perspicacious proofreader Jennifer McClain, marvelous and pioneering marketing and publicity team David Hawk and Windy Dorresteyn, and the rest of the terrific Ten Speed Press staff.

INTRODUCTION

> Words bounce. Words, if you let them, will do what
> they want to do and what they have to do.
>
> —ANNE CARSON, *AUTOBIOGRAPHY OF RED*

This book is about words that aren't doing what they want to do because we're not letting them. It's really a word liberation book—letting those words be the words they were meant to be.

It's about how we misuse the English language and use the wrong words that don't mean what we think they mean. It's not only about mistakes, but about correcting those mistakes, and discussing if they're even mistakes at all. In short, it's about the 150 most commonly confused, abused, questioned, and misused words and phrases in the English language, according to surveys, dictionaries like *Merriam-Webster's*, usage panels like the *American Heritage* panel, and top word experts like Steven Pinker and Bryan Garner. Each entry includes examples of word misuse from the media along with short histories of how and why these mistakes have happened, as well as some of the (often surprisingly nasty) debates about which uses are mistakes, which aren't, and, finally, how to use these words correctly.

These are the words that educated people most often misuse, are embarrassed about misusing, and want to use correctly. Some of them are what are sometimes called *bubble words*—words of which you are sure you know the meaning, but you actually don't. Others are *homophones*—members of the always confusing sound-alike-but-mean-different group. Still others are *paronyms*, or what some people more colloquially call "confusables" because, yes, they're confusing on account of they sound similar (like *mitigate* and *militate* or *discomfit* and *discomfort*) but yet again mean different things.

These are all different forms of *catachresis*—the technical term for saying something that doesn't mean what you think it means.

Before we begin, we want to say emphatically that we're not absolute, antiquarian-style prescriptivists who speak in funny quasi-British accents, stare over our glasses, and insist on old definitions of words and refuse to acknowledge changes in English. Nor are we snotty grammar nazis who delight in catching people in mistakes. For one thing, we've made mistakes ourselves—and it would be more than hypocritical to criticize other people for doing what we've done. And after all, the latest *Oxford English Dictionary* (*OED*) lists 171,476 words in current usage (and another 47,156 obsolete words). That's a myriad, plethora, staggering number, enormity, or (as *Merriam-Webster's* notes is "a vulgar usage") a real shitload of words. True, many of them are words most of us don't use—like *amphibology* (a grammatically ambiguous phrase), *anguilliform* (resembling an eel), or *zetetic* (investigation), but the point is that it's impossible for anyone to be fully conversant with all the words in English, or even the most common ones, and use each one of them correctly. We found examples of mistaken usage from national newspapers such as the *New York Times* and *Washington Post*, from eminent authors and magazines, as well as from blogs, Wikipedia, newscasts, and popular magazines. So yeah, we ALL make mistakes.

More to the point, words change, times change, and meanings change, and we're not about to halt the flow of time. (Especially because we can't.) We're not going to be *struthious* (resembling an ostrich) and stick our heads in the sand. Take an obvious example: the word *gay*. In medieval times, it meant not only "full of joy" but also "wanton" and "lewd." By the 1890s, a "gay house" meant a "brothel," and a "gay cat" a "hobo," but the general use was still cheerful—a 1940s best seller, *Our Hearts Were Young and Gay*, talked about happy young people with no sexual preference overtones whatsoever. But as we all know now in the twenty-first century, *gay* means, well, *gay*, "someone with a sexual preference for the same sex." In most cases, there's no going back with words and new meanings. It's not a bold prediction to say that "gay" will eventually completely lose its meaning of "cheerful." Words are peripatetic: they don't stay put, they boldly forge ahead, no matter how hard we try to hold them back.

But—and there's always a "but" with words and word usage—sometimes words are misused in a way that hinders communication, confuses issues, and generally makes language less clear than it should be. Those are the words we primarily chose for this book. Unless you're an obscure poet or a chairperson of the Federal Reserve (who mostly gets the economy wrong anyway), we think you should strive to make language—and obviously the words you choose—clear and succinct. That's the goal of using language—to communicate ideas and desires in the clearest way possible.

But—and there's always *another* "but" with language—who gets to decide what's right and wrong? France has a national academy, the Académie française, that rules on what's good

French and what's not. English is more democratic: we all decide. We yell, argue, talk, and write, and eventually some sort of consensus is reached; and then, of course, things change once more. Naturally, in different parts of the English-speaking world, different words are sometimes considered correct. You want to "prepone" a meeting? You don't say that in the United States, but it's considered correct by many in India. This book is about what's generally considered correct right now by educated people in the generally accepted standard dialect of North America called GA (General American). We try to tack (not "tact"—see page 175) our way through the stormy seas of linguistic confusion and arrive at reasonable conclusions of what to say and what not to say. We throw in a little word history and etymology as well. It's designed to be fun, but it's also designed to educate. Most of all, it's designed to give you some "word armor" in speaking and writing.

Like it or not, words can be dangerous, humiliating, and anger inducing. People can get absolutely infuriated over words. Just recently in an online argument over politics, a writer criticized someone over the "tenants of his beliefs." The guy fired back and ridiculed the writer for choosing the wrong word—it should have been "tenets," and instead of talking about the criticism (in our opinion justified), the internet was buzzing with talk about the "dumb" guy (that's the most polite pejorative, you can imagine the others) who couldn't write English correctly. It was unfair, and detracted from an important debate, but it happened. And that's also why we wrote this book, so it doesn't happen to you; or in a lesser way, so people don't simply look at you quizzically when you use the wrong word. Who wants to sound like they don't know what they're talking about? (Hint: rhetorical question.)

But most of all, words are fun. It's fascinating to delve into the complicated histories of words and see how they came to mean what they do. As Steve Martin once said, "Some people have a way with words, and other people . . . oh, uh, not have way." This book is for all of us, who at least occasionally, uh, "not have way" with words.

Three quick notes: This book is a collection of misused words (and some nonwords) in alphabetical order, as well as, in many cases, the words they're confused with. When there are pairs (or triplets), the first word listed is the one most often misused.

Due to space considerations, we were unable to include citations for examples and quotes in the book itself. They are listed on our website, www.kandrpetras.com.

At the end of each entry, we've included very basic definitions of the misused and often confused words, along with, when applicable, the words they're confused with. Note the previous adjective *basic*. (And, while we're at it, note the adverb *very*.) Most of these words have many forms, definitions, and nuances; the basic definitions that we include are there just to clarify our discussions and show contrasting meanings. For more detailed definitions, of course, there's the dictionary!

a priori

"Setting an a priori date for the event, however, would be dangerous."

—UNITED NATIONS PRESS RELEASE

The United Nations has fallen into a common trap . . . and you Kant really blame them. Ever read philosopher Immanuel Kant and his *Critique of Pure Reason*? We haven't either, and thus begins most of the confusion with *a priori* for nonphilosophers.

It seems like everyone except for a few Kantians thinks that *a priori* is a fancy way of saying "prior" or "beforehand," as in the example above. It isn't. Yes, *a priori* in the original Latin means "from the former" or "in advance." But thanks to Kant and other philosophers, it now means something more specific and confusing in English and other modern languages.

Loosely speaking, *a priori* means "knowledge or things that we already know, not based on experiment, but deduced from axioms," i.e., knowledge that is accepted or established. In other words, you can have a priori knowledge of mathematical notions like 2+2=4 (Socrates had a famous demonstration of this when he showed how an illiterate slave implicitly "understood" geometry), but you can't have a priori knowledge of the results of a football game because you don't know which team will score and how often. (And just to be technical, Kant says that our knowledge of mathematics is both a priori *and* synthetic. But let's not go there.) On the other hand, *a posteriori*, which also comes from Latin, means "what comes after" and is used in philosophy to mean reasoning from known facts, experiments, or experience. Our advice: unless you're a philosopher, don't use either.

a priori (adj): based on axiomatic reasoning and deduction

---

abjure / adjure

"[Joanne] Stepaniak offers a code of vegan ethics: (1) Vegans are sensitive to issues of suffering, (2) vegans value awareness of all life forms, (3) vegans adjure violence, and (4) vegans expand the principle of harmlessness."

—*THE RHETORIC OF FOOD*

Violent vegans?

Adjure means "to require, often under oath, to earnestly urge." So vegans adjuring violence means they're getting their pitchforks ready and sharpened for an attack.

Doubtful, whatever you may think of veganism. The authors (we hope) meant *abjure*, which means "to solemnly reject or renounce." So vegans are not on the rampage, but instead are rejecting violence.

It's an important distinction, of course. The difference between *abjure* and *adjure* is simple—it's all a matter of going toward or going away from. (Both words are from Latin, as are 28.34 percent of all English words, according to a survey by the compilers of the *Shorter Oxford Dictionary*. How's that for specificity!) The "jure" part of both words is from *jurare* (to swear an oath). The big question is, are you *going away from* the oath or *moving toward* making it? *Ab-* in Latin is a prefix meaning "away," so *ab*jure is walking away from swearing an oath, renouncing a solemn promise, or rejecting something. *Ad-* in Latin is a prefix meaning "to," so *ad*jure means "to require, urge, or command," as in requiring someone to adhere to the oath he or she made.

Confusing *abjure* and *adjure* is easy. That's probably why both words so often appear on the SATs, GMATs, and other standardized tests. And, except for students of Latin, it's also easy to forget the difference once those horrible days of test taking are happily in the past. But it's just a matter of *ad-* (to) and *ab-* (away).

abjure (v): to renounce solemnly
adjure (v): to earnestly request someone to do something

---

abrogate / arrogate

"The state has effectuated a coup, as it now has abrogated to itself the authority once belonging to the Church universal."
—AMERICAN THINKER

The American Thinker should have done some more thinking. Instead of *abrogated*, the Thinker should have used *arrogated*. Confusing these words is easy even for self-styled (lowercase) thinkers like us.

Abrogate basically means "to abolish or repeal a law." It's a *giving away* word. The American Thinker was talking about the state *taking up*—as in *arrogate*, meaning "to claim something, usually without justification," as in this quote about the government grabbing authority that once belonged to the Church. (People have been complaining about this sort of thing for generations, like this from 1627: "King Henry the VIII . . . purposed . . . to arrogate vnto himselfe the title of head of the Church of England." Notice they (correctly) used *arrogate*. Then again, power-hungry Henry VIII would never have abrogated any of his legal authority ever.)

Both words came from Latin into English, and the big difference between the two comes from those old Latin prefixes that we mentioned earlier: *ab-* and *ad-* (the *d* got melded into the *r* in *arrogate*). *Arrogate*'s *ad-* means "to" or "toward," and *-rogate* comes from *rogare* (to ask), so it means "moving to ask," or "claiming something," as with King Henry or the state grabbing authority. The *ab-* in *abrogate* means "away," and *-rogate* here means "to propose a law." So *abrogate* means "moving *away* from the law, or abolishing it." Similar *ab-* (away) words are *abnegate*, "to renounce or reject something desirable," and *abdicate*, "to give up power," something many English people wanted Henry VIII to do after all of his annoying arrogating.

abrogate (v): to abolish or repeal a law, evade responsibility
arrogate (v): to claim something, usually without justification

---

adverse / averse

"Cat Has an Averse Reaction to Liquid in Commercial Food"
—HEADLINE, *WASHINGTON POST*

And we're having an *adverse* reaction to that *WaPo* headline—which is missing a crucial *d*. There's no such thing as an averse reaction . . . or, for that matter, averse weather, averse effects, or averse events, all of which we've recently seen in print.

So what's the big diff between them? Usually, a person is *averse* about something (we're *averse* to giving advice), whereas a thing is *adverse*. And usually, if it comes right before a noun, it should be *adverse* and not *averse*. The opposite holds as well: *averse* often comes after the noun, as in "People of retirement age are risk averse—they turn away from risk."

That said, people have been confusing *averse* and *adverse* for years, and we can blame it all on the Romans. It (probably) began with one Latin word, *vertere* (to turn). The Romans tacked those pesky prefixes *ad-* and *ab-* (here we go again . . .) onto *vertere* to mean two different things. The *ad-* version spawned *advertere*, "to turn toward," which evolved into *adverse*, "turning toward an enemy or a problem." The *ab-* version meant "turning away." Over time the *b* was dropped, so the word became *avertere*, *aversus*, and, finally, *averse*.

Nice and easy, but the descendants of the Romans, including the English, kept getting the two words confused, leading to the adverse use of averse, which still persists. At least we no longer use *averse* to mean "behind" or "in the rear," as in Sir Thomas Browne's famous *1650 Pseudodoxia epidemica*: "The situation of the genitalls is averse."

We'll refrain from further comments.

adverse (adj): not favorable, harmful
averse (adj): opposed to or strongly disliking

affect / effect

"The recent roller coaster weather has had an affect on wildlife in the area."

—FOX11ONLINE.COM

"This woman practiced gratitude for a year and was stunned by how it effected her health."

—BUSINESS INSIDER

It should have been the opposite in the examples above. According to Barron's, one of the largest SAT preparation courses, switching *effect* and *affect* is one of the most common errors students make . . . and it's not only students getting confused. So let's *effect* a change and correctly *affect* our speech.

Affect is almost always a verb meaning "to act upon, to make a change to something." The first example above should say that the woman "was stunned by how it *affected* her health." On the other hand, *effect* is usually a noun, and typically means "a change that resulted from something else acting on it."

Nice and neat . . . except that, as is so often the case with English, it gets a little more complicated (and annoying). *Affect* can also be used as a noun (most commonly in psychiatry, meaning an emotional response or state, as in "a flat affect"), and *effect* can be used as a verb, meaning "to cause a change to something."

With all this confusion between *affect* and *effect*, you'd think they both probably came from the same old root words, but they probably didn't. *Affect* mostly likely comes from the Latin *afficere*, meaning "to treat, to afflict." It was often used in a negative sense in early English, as in being affected or afflicted with some disease. *Effect* probably comes from another Latin word, *efficere* (to accomplish). Along the way from Latin through French to English, the two words and their derivations got tangled up in use and meaning, all to a bad effect today.

affect (v): to have an effect on
effect (n): a change caused by actions; (v): to cause something to happen

---

all together / altogether

"Bully anyone at anytime, and if someone asks you to stop, then you are just being—altogether now—politically correct."

—*THE NATION*

All together now—*altogether* and *all together* aren't the same. In fact, it's altogether wrong to write "altogether now." Confusing them is a problem that goes back many years, with the *Oxford English Dictionary* (*OED*) noting "altogethers" when "all togethers" would have been correct back in the 1700s.

Altogether is an adverb meaning "completely, entirely, totally," as in "It was altogether confusing." It first appeared in Old English as *altogedere* and over the years was used as a noun, adjective, and adverb with meanings revolving around the concept of the whole. (There's also *altogether* used as a noun as in "in the altogether" that means being nude, a usage that didn't emerge until 1894, but it isn't confused with *all together*.) The current adverbial meaning of *altogether* was actually one of the original meanings. The *OED* lists several examples of early usages, like this one written in 1225: "Here fifealde mihte was altegeder attred."

All together, on the other hand, is a phrase that means "in one place" or "all at once"—"The dancers arrived all together for the audition." Everyone or everything is being acted upon at the same time or is acting in unison. It isn't a simple adverb like *altogether*. And when used correctly, you can separate the "all" from the "together" and it will still make sense: "All the dancers arrived together for the audition."

That wasn't altogether too complicated, was it? (You don't have to answer all together.)

all together (phrase): in one place, all at once
altogether (adv): completely, totally

---

allude / elude

"During the call, Top Dawg threatened that Interscope and Universal Music Group (UMG) would take down the song, he eluded to possible legal action and took a highly aggressive stance."

—*XXL MAGAZINE*

No, Top Dawg *alluded* to possible legal action. *Elude* means "to evade, avoid detection," as in "Top Dawg eluded the fans pursuing him." *Allude* means "to mention in an indirect way, to hint at," as in what should have been written in the example above: "Top Dawg alluded to possible legal action."

Interestingly (and confusingly), *allude* and *elude* once had different meanings than their meanings today. Both words come from the Latin word for play or teasing—*ludere*—with prefixes tacked on. In medieval England, *allude* meant "to mock," and all through the 1500s and 1600s it also meant "to make puns," and was used frequently in this sense (although even early on it could also mean "to refer to" and "to hint at"). The medieval "teasing" meanings seem to make more sense given its Latin connection with playing, but, gradually, the meaning of "hinting at" took hold and allusions to punning were lost forever.

As for *elude*, in early English it sometimes meant "to delude," as well as "to baffle and disappoint"—as in this somewhat chilling sentence from 1594: "A witch or hagg is she which being eluded by a league made with the devil." This was written during the height of the terrible witch-hunting craze in England under James I. One only hopes the "witches or haggs" referred to literally eluded (in the later sense of evading) burning at the stake. Fortunately for those of us baffled by these definitions, by the early 1600s, *elude* firmed up its present meaning of evading and lost most of its other meanings. Even more fortunately for humanity, the witch-hunting craze ended in England, albeit a bit later, by 1716, when the last purported "witch" was executed.

allude (v): to mention in an indirect way
elude (v): to evade

---

allusion / illusion

". . . the way it catches the light, can magically create an allusion more powerful than the real thing."

—*LOS ANGELES TIMES*

In this mention of Japanese Noh theater, the *Los Angeles Times* should have just said, er, noh to *allusion*.

Yes, they have fallen prey to a very common mistake. *Allusion* and *illusion* are separated only by a single vowel, so it's no wonder they're so often confused. More often, the mistake is using *allusion* when *illusion* is called for. But they are definitely not interchangeable. An *allusion* is an indirect reference to something; an *illusion* is a misinterpreted reality, often a trick.

Where *allusion* is concerned, the key is "indirect." People also misuse the word by using it to mean an explicit or obvious reference. Allusion comes from the Latin *allusio*, meaning "game or play on words," and evolved to its current meaning in the 1600s.

Illusion, on the other hand, came from the French *illusion* by way of the Latin *illusion*, meaning "mocking or jeering."

So it is clear the two are distinct. For that reason, we will refrain from making an allusion to anything that gives you the illusion that these two words are the same, even though they look so similar. Got it? (Look, be glad we didn't throw *elusion*, meaning "escape or avoidance," into the mix. But this noun that stems from the verb *elude* isn't very commonly used. So let's forget all about it.)

allusion (n): indirect reference to something
illusion (n): wrongly perceived appearance, belief, or impression

---

alright / all right

"It's Alright, Ma, I'm Only Bleeding"
—BOB DYLAN SONG TITLE

No, it's not alright. Really, it isn't. And Cheap Trick's "We're All Alright" is all wrong.

It's *all right*. Well, according to standard English, that is. It's two words. Even though *alright* has been used by such literary heavyweights as James Joyce, Flannery O'Connor, and Gertrude Stein. It is so common nowadays that it is included in several dictionaries, such as the ever-inclusive *Merriam-Webster's*, which comments that alright "has its defenders and its users," and notes that "it is less frequent than *all right* but remains common especially in informal writing." The *New Oxford Dictionary* and *American Heritage Dictionary* similarly comment that alright is used widely, but is "nonstandard." So *alright* isn't all right? Not if you want to go along with style guides (like the *Columbia Guide to Standard American English* or the *AP Stylebook*).

Interestingly, the one-word *alright* is not a result of relaxing language standards. It actually appeared back in the twelfth century, spelled *alrihtes* or *alriht*, but with a different meaning (exactly) and was used spelled as it is today in 1664 as a sentence-ending "indeed!" Its use as a variant of *all right* didn't happen until 1893. And then, as it is now, it was more commonly used only in dialogue, quotations, or casual speech.

Alright supporters (and there are many) point out that it's just another word formed from "all" and a second word, like *altogether*, so is clearly acceptable. But *all together* and *altogether* mean two different things (see page 12), so the argument isn't quite as pat as all that. So let's stick with *all right*. All right?

all right (adj, adv): okay, satisfactory

alternate / alternative

"But in practice, what Rotten Tomatoes does is eliminate the distinction between genuine passion and lukewarm acceptance—or, alternately, the distinction between lukewarm dislike and passionate hatred."

—GQ

Speaking of passionate hatred, that's how many people feel about the use of *alternately* instead of *alternatively*. This is because, as with so many other confused words, while they sound alike, they technically don't mean the same thing.

They both come from the classic Latin *alternatus* (to do one thing and then another), but branched off onto different but related paths. And according to their strict meaning, *alternate* refers to two or more things happening one after another. *Alternative* means "another choice or possibility." But people use them interchangeably nowadays and, in fairness, there is most definitely a precedent, but a confusing one.

The *Oxford English Dictionary*'s (*OED*) earliest citation for the adjective *alternative*, dating from 1540, uses the term to mean "alternate." And the *OED*'s entry for the adjective *alternate* has citations going back to 1776, for the word used to mean, yup, "alternative." No wonder some people and dictionaries think that being strict about using *alternate* as *alternative* is a waste of time. Granted, after those initial switched meanings, the two words settled into their grooves and meant two different things. But as time has passed, they've gotten blurred.

Since *alternate* has become (sometimes grudgingly) an accepted alternative to *alternative*, you can use it as such and probably won't be chided. But if you want to please the purists, we suggest you use *alternative* as an alternate.

alternate (v, adj, n): refers to two or more things happening one after another
alternative (adj, n): another choice or possibility

---

ambivalent

"Don't Be Ambivalent About Ambivalence

So let's first acknowledge that we all have at least some degree of ambivalence. Since life itself is such an extremely complex process, and certain aspects of it often get more complicated as they evolve, a certain amount of ambivalence is actually normal."

—HUFFINGTON POST

We're definitely not ambivalent about the above writer's use of *ambivalent*. He seems to think, as do so many others, that ambivalent means being indifferent or not caring, saying "meh," in effect, to something or someone. But *ambivalent* actually means "being of two minds about something, being torn between two opposite attitudes, having contradictory feelings at the same time," which is something we're not about the meaning of this word.

It began as a purely psychological term, conceived in 1910 by Swiss psychiatrist Eugen Bleuler who combined the Latin *ambi-* (both) and *valentia* (strength) to come up with the noun form, *ambivalenz*. It first appeared as a direct anglicization of the original German term in printed English in a translation of Carl Jung's papers published in 1916: "Tendencies, under the stress of emotions, are balanced by their opposites—thus giving an ambivalent character to their expression." By the late 1920s, *ambivalence* had spilled over into nontechnical usage such as in Bertrand Russell's 1929 *Marriage and Morals* ("Christianity . . . has always had an ambivalent attitude towards the family.")

But between then and now, the meaning of *ambivalent* has blurred. Not only is it often used instead of *indifferent*, there also is a rising trend to use it in place of *ambiguous*. But there is nothing ambiguous (questionable, indistinct) about *ambivalence*'s true meaning. Sadly, many people and media outlets might not agree. When we did a quick search on Google news using it as the search term, we found six out of the first ten items used *ambivalent* incorrectly. Tsk tsk. What would Eugen Bleuler say?

ambivalent (adj): being of two minds about something, having contradictory feelings

---

ameliorate

"A couple of blocks away from the shelter, lawmakers on Capitol Hill this year passed a budget in which massive cuts were quietly made to the programmes that attempt to ameliorate the number of Americans sleeping rough or moving from place to place."

—*THE GUARDIAN*, US EDITION

Ameliorate means "to make better." So let's ameliorate our knowledge about the word.

All too often, as in the example above, people think *ameliorate* means "to lessen." This mistake is very common: doing a quick Google search, we found hundreds of phrases in which *ameliorate* was used when *lessen*, *reduce*, or *alleviate* should have been used instead.

It comes from the Latin word *melior* (better), via the Old French word *ameillorer* (modern French students probably know the later French word *meilleur*). Interestingly, in early modern English, the preferred form was without the *a*—*meliorate*—as in "Religion is to meliorate the condition of a people" (Bishop Taylor, 1647), but unless you want to sound like an antiquarian snob, stick with the *a* in *ameliorate*.

A quick linguistic note: In linguistics, *amelioration* is a technical word for a semantic change in which a word's meaning improves over time. For example, in early medieval times, *nice* meant "clumsy, poor, or weak" and later "stupid, foolish." But by the 1800s, it had undergone such extensive amelioration that it now meant "kind and thoughtful." The linguistic opposite of amelioration is pejoration. *Awful*, which used to mean "worthy of awe" underwent pejoration and today it means "very bad." Interestingly, *pejoration* is much more common in English than *amelioration*. Maybe it's time for a new linguistic superhero to ameliorate the language and alleviate the level of pejoration. We might call him or her the Awful Ameliorator. Or maybe not.

ameliorate (v): to improve something, usually to make something bad better

THE E.G. AND I.E. PROBLEM:
I.E., PEOPLE USING THEM WRONG,
E.G., THIS USAGE OF E.G.

Many usually grammatically sound writers think that e.g. and i.e. , both abbreviations for Latin phrases, are happily interchangeable. Many usually grammatically sound writers are wrong.

E.g. is the abbreviation for the Latin phrase *exempli gratia* (literally "for example"), which is, logically, what it means, as in a sentence like this: "Sometimes people who should know better, e.g., the writers of this book, misuse Latin abbreviations."

I.e. is the abbreviation for *id est* (that is) and means "in other words," as in "Sometimes people who should know better misuse Latin abbreviations, i.e., they have problems remembering which is which."

Both abbreviations have been used (and misused) in English for many years. According to the *OED*, *e.g.* appeared in a 1682 book and *i.e.* even earlier, in 1662.

To remember when you use each of them, here's a simple trick: The first letter tips you off. It's *e* for "example" in e.g. (or you could get a little cute and take the first two letters' sound—egg-sample) and *i* for "in other words" in i.e.

amenable / amendable

"Keanu Reeves has reestablished himself among the modern action heroes, which made fans wonder if there will be *The Matrix 4*. Reeves told the press that he was amendable to the idea of a fourth film in the franchise, but only if the original directors, the Wachowskis, will handle the movie.

—MSTARS NEWS

No, Keanu was *amenable*, not *amendable*. *Amendable* means "capable of being changed by additions or amendments," as in "The US Constitution is amendable." (We'd rather not amend Keanu. He seems fine the way he is.) *Amenable*, on the other hand, means "responsive, liable (in law), open to suggestions or ideas," as in "Keanu was amenable to the idea of a fourth film."

Amenable is a much more common and more useful word than *amendable* (unless you're a constitutional scholar). The Google Ngram, which measures word usage, shows that in recent years *amenable* was used seventy-five times more frequently than *amendable*.

While we're at it with *amendable*, it's also useful to distinguish the root verb *amend* from the similar sounding *emend*. *Amend* means "to improve, make better, to revise," whereas *emend* . . . quite often means the same thing! That said, *emend* usually refers to a literary text ("The copy editor emended the author's manuscript"), whereas *amend* tends to be broader in context. So while laws can be emended (minor corrections), they are usually amended. This confusion and similarity between the two words arises because both come from the same Latin root word *emendare* (to free from faults). But there is one clear distinction: the noun form of *amend* is *amendment*; the noun form of *emend* is not "emendment" but *emendation*. So we might (correctly but confusingly) say, "The copy editor was amenable to making emendations to the text of the amendment."

amenable (adj): open to suggestion, receptive
amendable (adj): able to be changed by amendments

amiable / amicable

"Amicable Woman with Eager Smile"
—PHOTO CAPTION, NPR.ORG

We'll smile when we say it: *amicable* doesn't really work to describe a person. *Amiable* does. *Amiable* means "having a friendly disposition," one that causes people to like you, while *amicable* is used to describe friendly relationships *between* people, not the people themselves. An amiable person can have an amicable relationship, but that person shouldn't be called amicable.

Amiable came to English first in the late fourteenth century from the Old French *amiable,* which came from the Latin *amicabilem* (friendly), from *amicus* (friend, loved one), from *amare* (to love). Nice and neat . . . except the meaning of *amiable* got mixed up with the Old French *amable* (lovable), which also derived from the Latin *amare,* by way of *amabilem* (lovable). So *amiable* began being used also to mean "inspiring love, especially due to being friendly and agreeable."

Because *amiable* had been muddied, in the early fifteenth century, *amicable* emerged, directly from the Latin form, to circumvent the French *amable* confusion. It initially meant simply "pleasant," but now is used to mean "free from hard feelings, harmonious."

An amicable conclusion if you ask us. (And even if you don't.)

amiable (adj): having a friendly disposition
amicable (adj): friendly, characterized by good will, harmonious (usually referring to relationships)

---

anchors away / anchors aweigh

"As the band played the familiar strains of 'The Marine Corps Hymn' or 'Anchors Away,' the US Navy song, members of each respective branch stood and were applauded."

—*OMAHA* [NE] *WORLD-HERALD*

Who can resist the familiar strains of "Anchors Away"? Well, we can. Not because we have anything against the navy, but because there is no such song nor such a saying, for that matter. It's "Anchors *Aweigh*," which sounds exactly the same, but is spelled differently and means something different entirely.

It's easy to see how it gets confused. "Anchors away" looks so logical. You can imagine an old salt yelling the order to cast off the rope and sail away. And it has been a source of confusion for centuries. The phrase shows up in 1627, in Captain John Smith's *A Sea Grammar*—the first known published use of the term at all—"What is the Anchor away?"

We can't answer that question, but we can answer another: why "aweigh" and not "away"? The "weigh" doesn't mean to determine the weight of. It's the same "weigh" as in "weigh anchor," that is, "to lift the anchor from the bottom." So when an anchor is aweigh, it's up. It's typical sailor parlance, this adding of an *a-* prefix to a word, which is how we got words like ashore, aboard, afloat, aground, and adrift.

This weigh/way confusion also goes the other way (sorry) in the case of "under way" (in motion). In nautical lingo, spelling it "under *weigh*," which evolved from confusion with the concept of weighing anchor, became common enough that it's considered a variant spelling. Herman Melville used it in his *Moby-Dick*, and it has also been used by such nonnautical authors as William Makepeace Thackeray, Washington Irving, and Charles Dickens. But it's best to say it's "under way" when you weigh anchor.

anchors aweigh (phrase): refers to weighing (lifting) anchor

---

apocryphal

"For many, it was an apocryphal moment. One which will be remembered for a lifetime."

—USA TODAY NETWORK'S "THE BAXTER REPORT"

We suspect it was a moment to remember, not a moment of doubtful or questionable authenticity, which is what *apocryphal* means.

Apocryphal usually refers to something that is widely repeated or disseminated as if it is true, even though it might not be. Over time, it also has come to mean "fictitious, false, mythical," definitions that now appear in numerous dictionaries (including the venerable *Oxford English Dictionary*) and ones that only the most nit-picking grammarian would take issue with.

Apocryphal emerged in the fourteenth century, springing from the Latin *apocrypha*, referring to noncanonical biblical books, from the Greek *apokryphos* (hidden), out of *apokruptein* (hide away). Over time, its meaning grew to also cover things that were false or unreal, as in Ben Jonson's 1612 comedy, *The Alchemist*: "A whoresonne, vpstart, Apocryphall Captayne."

Nice and neat, right? So what is *apocryphal* doing in here? Well, for some reason, over the past decade or so, people have begun using it in the phrase "an apocryphal moment" to refer not to a spurious moment but to an "aha" moment or a momentous moment, if you will. In other words, somehow something apocryphal has gotten confused with something epiphanic.

We'd say it's apocalyptic, but that's yet another word that *apocryphal* is lately being confused with.

apocryphal (adj): something probably not true but often believed to be

---

appraise / apprise

"In a statement to the *New York Post*, a CBS spokeswoman denied Chris Simms's claims, saying the network kept both Phil Simms and his agent appraised of his situation.

—MSN NEWS

When popular NFL commentator Phil Simms was bumped out of his broadcasting booth, his son Chris Simms angrily complained, but CBS claimed that they had kept Phil "appraised of the situation." *Appraise* means "to decide the value of." Why would Chris Simms complain that his dad wasn't being constantly kept up to date on his value? No, we're going to take a not-so-wild guess and assume that what CBS meant to say was that they *informed* Phil. And lo and behold, there's a word that sounds a lot like *appraise* that actually means "to inform," which, you guessed it, is *apprise*. (When you think about it, in one sense CBS also *appraised* Phil Simms—they decided his value to the network, but that's maybe going a little too far.)

Confusing the two words is a fairly common problem: we've found midwives appraising mothers about their babies, computer users being appraised of their progress, and politicians being appraised of the latest polls. Frankly, in all cases, "informed" would do just as well, but *apprised* would also be correct (and *appraised* wouldn't be).

The opposite case of using *apprise* for *appraise* is rarer but certainly not uncommon. Wanna buy a painting apprised for $3000? You can at Peterson Antiques. And the Lender's Network informs us of how to calculate a loan based on the "apprised market value of a property." Careless errors? Maybe. But let's strive to keep things straight, and for paintings or homes, you can be apprised of their appraised values but you can't be appraised of their apprised values. At least not in this universe.

appraise (v): to establish a value, estimate an amount
apprise (v): to give information

ascent / assent

"Spectators watching the assent of the balloon *Ben Franklin*"
—BRYN MAWR COLLEGE LIBRARY PHOTOGRAPH COLLECTION

Even academics do it: confuse *assent* and *ascent*. *Assent* is a verb meaning "to express approval," and *ascent* is a noun meaning "a climb." Balloons make an ascent; they don't make an assent (unless they're exceptionally agreeable balloons).

Ascent comes from the Latin words *ad-* (to) and *scandere* (climb). *Assent* comes from the Latin *ad-* and *sentire* (think). Clear differences in origin, clear differences in current meanings.

Yet they are often confused. In most cases, this seems to be due more to carelessness or preoccupied minds than not knowing the difference between the words. But there are other cases where we think otherwise; and we found some strange misspelled hybrids of the two words, such as this in Lewis and Clark's famous journals: "Some time e'er, we found the proper road which assends a high mountain" (Clark, September 15, 1805). In fact, we found a number of cases where Lewis and Clark were busily "assending [approving of and climbing simultaneously?] mountains," too many instances to be simple careless errors. Lewis and Clark should have, of course, been *ascending* (climbing) mountains as proper explorers do. But in these pre-Webster's dictionary days, spelling wasn't standardized, so the *c*'s and *s*'s in these words or the lack thereof don't seem to have mattered much.

We live here and now though, in an era graced with advanced spell-checking programs, and should tenaciously stick with the proper spellings and usages. So we leave you with this wish: may you assent to our recommendations in this, and ascend to a high level of linguistic prowess.

ascent (n): a climb or going into the air like a balloon
assent (v): to agree to

assure / ensure / insure

"He was scared to see me again and I ensured him as long as he had good intentions, nothing bad would happen."

—NOVEL (PUBLISHED 2014) FOUND ON GOOGLE BOOKS

In the spirit of support for novice writers, we're not naming names, particularly because this is only one of hundreds (we quit counting at one thousand) of wrong uses of *ensure*.

Ensure means "to make certain," as in "This law ensures that all banks will obey the law." *Assure* means "to reassure, to give confidence to someone." *Ensure* all too often pinch-hits for *assure*, as in the example above. But it's a linguistic strike-out. The problem with both words is that "sure" part—from the French *seur* and Latin *securus*, meaning "safe, secure." Tack on a few different prefixes and you've got different words meaning different things, although admittedly there's some overlap. It's just that often there's not enough overlap to allow for one to substitute for the other.

Then there's also *insure*, which *ensure* sometimes pinch-hits for. And this time most word umpires won't call a strike, although we recommend sticking to *insure* when you're talking about issuing a financial insurance policy. (Sometimes *assure* also pinch-hits for *insure*, which is why you sometimes see both "life insurance" and "life assurance" companies and policies.) But it's a lot easier to just stick with the basics. A linguistically inclined insurance professional demonstrates the three best usages in one sentence: "I assure you I will ensure that I insure my house."

assure (v): to reassure, give confidence to someone
ensure (v): to make certain
insure (v): to arrange for compensation for financial or other losses

baited breath / bated breath

"One would hope it's when you wait with baited breath or expect a photo of someone's child that common sense would kick in."
—TMZ.COM

Use the phrase "baited breath" and you're fishing for trouble. (Sorry for the dreadful pun. We can't worm our way out of it.)

It's *bated*. It has nothing to do with bait, hook, fish, or anything like that. The *bate* in *bated breath* came about in the fourteenth century when the word *abate* was shortened by *aphesis* (when a word loses its first unstressed vowel). So *abate* (to lessen) became *bate* and was used as such through the 1800s. It's no longer in use much at all, except in the phrase *bated breath*—a phrase used when someone is so affected by emotion, like awe or terror, that his breath gets short. It first appeared in published form in 1596, in William Shakespeare's *The Merchant of Venice*: "Shall I bend low and in a bondman's key / With bated breath and whispering humbleness / Say this. . . ."

So *bated breath* has quite a history. But many people make the mistake of using *bate*'s more familiar homophone "bait." It even appeared in one edition of *Harry Potter and the Prisoner of Azkaban*: "The whole common room listened with baited breath."

On the plus side, when we plugged both phrases into Google's Ngram Viewer (which charts usage in published books from 1800 to 2008), "bated breath" is used much more often. But there is one small negative: "baited breath" has been on an upswing since 2000. Will this continue? We'll wait with . . . you know.

bated breath (n): short breath due to extreme emotion

barter / haggle

"In some countries, vendors are less interested in the haggle. In general, shop owners are less likely to be bartered down than sellers in market booths."

—AIRTREKS WEBSITE, ON HAGGLING FOR RUGS

This is an interesting example. In the first sentence, the writer gets it right: when you're bargaining over the price of a rug, you're haggling. In the second sentence, the writer gets it wrong. Bartering is not haggling—it's trading, exchanging goods or services *without* using money. (Note: Of course you can haggle along with bartering; offering and counteroffering more or less goods or services in exchange for other goods or services.)

Confusing *haggling* with *bartering* is a common mistake, especially for Americans, maybe because most of us still don't like haggling or bartering all that much (even though that's changing.) We tend to go into a store, see a price, and pay it. And because we traditionally don't haggle and/or barter, we don't think about or really care about the distinctions.

Barter and *haggle* have unusual and unsavory pasts. *Haggle* initially meant, among other things, "to hack, mangle, and mutilate." As for *barter*, it comes from the Middle English *bartren,* from Old French *barater,* meaning "to barter," or, more notably, "to cheat." There are a slew of words centering around this concept—swindlers were called *baratours* in merrie olde England; in France, they were called *barateors*. Times have changed since then, but cheating hasn't, and a related word, *barratry,* is still in common use today in our law courts. It means "pursuing litigation for purposes of harassment or profit"—as by an ambulance-chasing lawyer, a baratour if we ever saw one.

barter (v): to trade by exchanging items instead of money
haggle (v): to bargain

begrudgingly / grudgingly

"'Martin Shkreli never intended to defraud anyone. . . . Investors who made millions will come here and begrudgingly admit they are not victims,' he told the jury."

—CNN.COM

This one is a hairsplitter, but should be mentioned because many people (read "sometimes overly didactic grammar types" and we will put ourselves grudgingly—but not begrudgingly— in that group) think that *begrudgingly* shouldn't be used when *grudgingly* is the better choice.

What's the difference other than that little *be-* prefix? First, let's look at that little *be-* prefix because it looms rather large. It changes the root verb *grudge* from an intransitive to a transitive verb. Because transitive verbs must have an object that receives whatever action you're doing, when you begrudge, you have to begrudge someone or something. (You can grudge all you want on your own.)

That's one key difference, but there's also a more nuanced difference in their meanings. When you do something *grudgingly*, you do it reluctantly. But *begrudgingly* typically has a more negative spin, since the verb it comes from, *begrudge*, has as its first and more common meaning "to envy (someone) the possession of something, to be dissatisfied with." So when you're doing something begrudgingly, usually you're not only doing it reluctantly, but also with a bad attitude.

Finally, *grudgingly* is the older of the two words—appearing back in 1549 according to the *OED*, while *begrudgingly*'s first entry comes from 1853. And speaking of the *OED* . . . it throws a wrench in the works, as its definition for *begrudgingly* is "in a grudging manner or spirit." (This, naturally, makes us want to hold quite a grudge against this august publication.)

begrudgingly (adv): in a dissatisfied, disapproving, or envious manner
grudgingly (adv): reluctantly

---

begs the question

"Mueller's special counsel appointment begs the question—
are our civil liberties now at risk?"

—COLUMN HEADLINE, FOXNEWS.COM

This headline begs a question itself: Is *begs the question* used correctly? Answer: Technically, no. And it's (technically) not used correctly in our sentence either.

In spite of popular thought and much to our surprise, *begs the question* is not a smart-sounding way of saying "raises the question" at all. Of course, if you have been using the phrase in that way, you're far from alone. An unscientific search on Google found more incorrect usages of "begs the question" than correct. In fact, of the first seventy-five citations of the phrase, not one was correct.

So what *is* correct? It's all very logical. Literally. *Begs the question* is a formal logic term, a translation of the Latin *petitio principii* (begging the question). In logic, this means you are trying to prove something based on a premise that needs to be proved itself. Like so much that is logical or philosophical, it sounds more complicated than it is. *Begging the question* is actually pretty clear: "French films are the best because they make films better in France." "They make films better in France" is an assumption that isn't supported in this sentence, so it doesn't prove that French films are better. It begs the question.

This raises a good question: Why, if you're talking about raising a question, use *beg the question* at all? To sound smart? Well, we think it's smarter to leave *beg the question* where it technically belongs, in the realm of logic and law, and just use the (correct) "raise the question" when that's what you're trying to say. It's a lot simpler (and clearer) that way.

begs the question (phrase): trying to prove something based on an unproved premise

---

bemused / amused

"Mr. Obama maintained a placid and at times bemused demeanor . . . as he parried the attacks."

—*NEW YORK TIMES*

Even the *New York Times* with its professional copy editors does it (and *Times* editors cop to it themselves, as the above example is cited in an article in their *After Deadline* blog)—using *bemused* as a presumably erudite way of saying amused. This bemuses us, because *bemused* does not mean "amused"; it means "to find something confusing or perplexing."

And speaking of confusing . . . *amused* initially meant pretty much what *bemused* means today. Back in the 1600s, *amused* meant "to be in a muse," i.e., distracted or absorbed. But from the mid-1700s on, it began primarily being used to mean "entertained." As for *bemused*, it first appeared in print in 1734 when poet Alexander Pope wrote of "a parson much bemus'd in beer." According to the *OED*, he meant that beer caused the so-called muse to descend upon the parson and inspire him to write, but lexicographers thought it meant "confused because of consumption of beer." Thus was born the current meaning.

But people who should know better keep using *bemused* as *amused*. When we did a quick Google search of news articles with *bemused* in their headlines, we found only one correct usage of it on the first page of results. Sigh. As Queen Victoria might say, we are not amused.

(Note: *Merriam-Webster's* does define *bemused* as "to cause to have feelings of wry or tolerant amusement." But it is one of the only major dictionaries to do so [and lists this meaning third].)

bemused (adj): lost in thought or confused
amused (adv): entertained

bimonthly / biweekly

> "When a newspaper is published 'bi-weekly', we receive two copies a week . . . but the *New York Journal of Medicine* comes to us once in two months instead of twice a month. If 'bi-weekly' means twice a week . . . why should 'bi-monthly' mean once in two months, and not twice a month?"
>
> —LETTER TO THE *SOUTHERN LITERARY MESSENGER*, 1844

Here's a confusing one. According to *Merriam-Webster's*, *biweekly* can mean either "occurring twice a week OR once every two weeks." Ditto for *bimonthly*. (At least there are *semiweekly* and *semimonthly*: they mean "twice a week" and "twice a month" . . . only.) Why the confusion?

It's all due to that pesky prefix *bi-*. As in *bisexual*, the *bi-* part clearly means "two." But for time, does the *bi-* mean twice in a given period or the given period times two? Well, it all depends. In the 1800s, *biweekly* usually meant "twice a week." But today *biweekly* almost always means "every two weeks." On the other hand, *biannual* usually means "twice in a year," yet *bicentennial* means "every two centuries," not twice in a century. It's enough to make the two of us scream—on more than a biweekly basis.

So what to do? Our suggestion: either use *semi-* to describe something twice in a given period or say "twice a month," etc. You could say *fortnightly* for every two weeks (it comes from fourteen nights), but that sounds a wee bit too British to us. For yearly periods, *biannual* is twice a year and *biennial* (usually) is every two years, but why not just say twice a year (or every six months) and every two years—and just say *bi*-bye to those *bi*-words?

bimonthly (adj): occurring every two months or twice a month
biweekly (adj): occurring every two weeks or twice a week

chronic

"Denis O'Brien, the largest shareholder at Independent News and Media (INM), said that the company is in an 'extremely chronic financial situation.'"

—*IRISH EXAMINER*

Talking about an "extremely chronic financial situation" isn't saying much except that it's lasting a long time, which isn't all that interesting. O'Brien meant that his company was in a very bad situation, which is interesting—especially to investors. (In fact, it was in dire financial straits and ultimately sold a large chunk of itself to bankers.)

All too often, people think *chronic* means bad, severe, or terrible. But it simply means something has happened or is happening over a long time period. True, *chronic* often has negative connotations, usually medical, and we hear and see it most often from people like a neighbor of ours complaining about terrible things like his chronic tennis elbow. But all the "chronic" part means is that it's lasted at least three months, according to commonly accepted medical definitions. The opposite of a chronic injury in medicine is *acute*, which is an injury that occurs suddenly, as in a traffic accident or a fall.

This distinction between *acute* and *chronic* using these very same two words (with a slight Latin twist) goes back to ancient Roman physician Caelius Aurelianus, who wrote the definitive medical textbook of the time, *De morbis acutis et chronicis* (*On Acute and Chronic Illnesses*), that every aspiring Roman doctor had to read. He got the Latin word *chronic* from the Greek Kronos, or Father Time as he became known in later eras.

Caelius Aurelianus laid out what *acute* and *chronic* meant, and we should always follow the doctor's orders.

chronic (adj): happening over a long time period

---

cliché / clichéd

"Changing rooms are so cliché: Courtney Stodden's pal strips in middle of shop."

—HEADLINE, *DAILY STAR* [UK]

This headline is wrong, and not because reality-show contestant and actress Courtney Stodden's pal stripped down to black underwear in the middle of the shop—which, incidentally, was probably not a good idea. We agree with the idea behind the headline, just not the choice of words.

See, *cliché* is a *noun*, not an adjective. It is a *thing*, not a descriptor. Saying "the changing rooms are so cliché" is like saying "the changing rooms are so platitude," or "the changing rooms are very overused phrase," because that's what *cliché* means.

The headline should have said changing rooms are so *clichéd*, an adjective describing the noun phrase "changing room." (FYI: Many adjectives, but by no means all, have -*ed* at the end and come from past participles of verbs—as in bored, from "to bore." That's not the case with *cliché*, which has no verb in English, although the adjective has the -*ed*).

Cliché used as an adjective (instead of *clichéd*) is virtually everywhere. Just type in "are so cliché" without a *d* in Google and you'll be horrified (if you love grammar) to find thousands of things that wrongly "cliché"—everything from store-bought flowers, cheese balls, groomsmen's gifts, balloons, chocolate, photos of pregnant women in nets (huh?), the Kardashians, possessed children in films, red roses, animated statues, and the Kardashians yet again. That's a lot of mistakes, so many, in fact, that this error is becoming a sort of a cliché (noun) in itself. But rants like this are so clichéd (adjective.)

cliché (n): something (usually a phrase or concept) that is trite or overused
clichéd (adj): referring to something that is trite or overused

---

climatic / climactic

"Be a Part of Cosmo's International Don't Fake It Day

On that Friday, we want you to stop pretending and actually have the climax you deserve . . . or at least fess up to your guy why it's been happening so you can work on a solution together. It's going to be one hell of a climatic day and we want you to be a part of it."

—*COSMOPOLITAN*

We really don't think *Cosmo* was referring to the weather in that last sentence. But that's exactly what *climatic* means, "relating to the climate." Was "International Don't Fake It Day" supposed to be a weather event? Nah, we'll take a wild guess and say it was supposed to be an orgasmic and *climactic* date with that extra *c* thrown in.

Climactic, as you may guess, comes (no pun intended) from *climax*. *Climax* means "culmination, the highest or most intense point of something." In *Cosmo* and elsewhere, it's often used in a sexual sense. *Climactic* is an adjectival form of *climax*, and to make it, the *x* is tossed out and a *ct* thrown in, followed by the adjective suffix -*ic*.

Climatic is another adjective. It comes from *climate*—and to make it, the *e* is tossed out and the suffix -*ic* is added. Easy enough, but all too often people put in this climate-related adjective where instead they should be using the climax-related adjective. This situation is even worse with the word *anticlimactic*, which means "causing disappointment after promising much in the way of a climax" (something *Cosmo* readers were probably fervently discussing after their "Don't Fake It Day"). With *anticlimactic*, the *c* is all too often forgotten and *anticlimatic* is written or said. But there's no *anticlimatic* in English. Although, when you think about it, with all the debates now going on about climate change, maybe there should be.

climatic (adj): referring to climate
climactic (adj): referring to climax

---

compel / impel

"Why an Australian Woman Felt Compelled to Go Door to Door Campaigning for Hillary Clinton

'So why did I volunteer to go door to door for Hillary Clinton one chilly morning in rural New Hampshire? . . . I figured, why not?'"

—*SYDNEY MORNING HERALD*

What's wrong with this headline? The Australian woman wasn't *compelled* to campaign at all. Neither Hillary Clinton nor her crew were at her back with guns or threats of blackmail (at least presumably). *Compelled* means "forced or obliged to do something," and the Australian clearly volunteered. Instead, she was *impelled* to campaign—"persuaded to take action on moral or ethical grounds." She liked Clinton and wanted to help out. Just to keep things bipartisan, an article on the Town Hall website titled "Why I Now Feel Compelled to Vote for Trump" is wrong for the same reasons—the author was not compelled but impelled to vote for Trump; no one was forcing him. To the best of our knowledge, Trump wasn't tweeting threats.

Both words come from Latin—*compel* meaning "to drive (usually a herd) together" and *impel* meaning "to drive (a herd) toward." The derivations aren't much help in determining differences. Maybe it's too bad that *compel* entered into English at all. Before the mid-1300s, there was another word, the native and evocative Middle English word *fordriven* (to drive out, to lead to, to compel, to force), that sounds, well, compelling—in fact, we'd be impelled to use it. But that word was fordriven—or driven out—by *compel* when it traveled with the Normans from France to England.

compel (v): to force or to oblige someone to do something
impel (v): to use moral pressure to persuade someone to do something

---

complacent / complaisant

"This interruption of the poliovirus circulation is significant, but we cannot afford to be complaisant."

—UNICEF PRESS RELEASE

We cannot afford to be complacent about that use of *complaisant*. It isn't a different way to spell *complacent* and the two words are not interchangeable.

Like so many easily confused words, they look similar and sound alike. They both evolved from the Latin word *complacere* (to please or to be pleasing) and both still have the concept of pleasing in their meanings.

Complacent is the more common of the two words and means "pleased with oneself, self-satisfied." *Complaisant* means "willing to please or yielding." In both cases, there is sometimes a slightly negative connotation implied: *complacent* being so smug that you ignore possible problems, *complaisant* being too prone to unquestioningly go along with others.

Complacent entered English in the late 1600s and initially meant simply "pleasing or pleasant." It began meaning "self-satisfied" about one hundred years later, and has retained that meaning. *Complaisant* came onto the scene at about the same time, but evolved from the Middle French *complaisant*, a form of *complaire* (acquiesce to please). Four hundred years later, it has still kept its French spelling, and its initial meaning.

So the two words are different, but there's a caveat. Some dictionaries, including Dictionary.com and *American Heritage*, list one of the definitions for *complacent* as . . . *complaisant*. But the *OED*, while including this definition (with a question mark), notes that it is obsolete. And we're standing with the *OED* on this one. Who wants to be obsolete?

complacent (adj): self-satisfied, often overly so
complaisant (adj): willing to please

"If you're competing for the title of 'favorite child' this Mother's Day, score major brownie points by bringing mom to Hooters for a complementary meal."

—RESTAURANTNEWS.COM

There's something wrong here. No, we don't mean that you won't become Mom's favorite by taking her to Hooters (although we have our doubts). We mean the meal, which isn't com*ple*mentary but com*pli*mentary.

Yes, here we have yet another duo of easily confused words separated by only one vowel. But it's a very important vowel, as it tells you just what each word means.

Complementary is the adjective derived from *complement* and, as such, describes things that complete one another, that combine to enhance each other's qualities. Its first use in this sense was in 1829, referring to complementary colors. *Complimentary* is the adjective derived from *compliment*, and describes things that convey praise or things that are free (for example, "compliments of the house"). It isn't really complicated if you pay attention. There's even a simple mnemonic to help: if *I* get something free, it's complimentary. Of course, there are moments when it's not quite as clear-cut. For example, a free glass of wine with a meal could be described as both complimentary and, if selected specifically to pair with the food, complementary. It's enough to drive you to drink—which reminds us of an apt, if dreadful, joke:

A man goes into a bar and hears a voice saying, "You look wonderful! Great haircut! Nice jacket!" But he looks around and he is the only person in the bar. The bartender walks over. "Oh, you're not going crazy. That's just the complimentary peanuts."

complementary (adj): of two or more things that combine to enhance each other

complimentary (adj): describing things that convey praise or given free as a courtesy

---

comprise

"As described by the Congressional Research Service, the committee would be comprised of members from the House and the Senate."

—*TIME*

"Comprised of." We have to admit that we say it, *Time* and the *New York Times* say it (sometimes), so does the *New Yorker*. Jimmy Carter said it, as did writers as diverse as Sue Monk Kidd, Anthony Trollope, Norman Mailer, Christopher Hitchens, Joyce Carol Oates, and Lionel Trilling. So what's the problem?

Well, it goes against the traditional correct usage—and logic. Traditionally, *comprise* is defined and used in the active sense to mean "to constitute, to consist of." More to the point, the *whole* comprises the parts and there's no "of"—as in "The house comprised five rooms." You shouldn't say, "The house is comprised of five rooms." That's the passive, and it's a big no-no to some who say we should use "composed of" or "consists of" instead. But times are changing. In the 1960s, more than half of the authoritative *American Heritage* Usage Panel disapproved of "comprised of," but by 2011 only 32 percent did. "Comprised of" has become an idiom. Who cares if it's technically incorrect?

But there are some valiant holdouts, notably famous (or infamous) software engineer Bryan Henderson who has made it his one-man mission to eradicate "comprise/s/d of" in all Wikipedia entries. Using a special bot, he finds the offending phrases and, on Sunday nights, replaces them—even in individual quotations from authors he thinks should know better. He's scoured five million Wiki pages thus far and has rid the encyclopedia of about fifty thousand "comprised ofs."

comprise (v): to consist of, be made up of

---

contiguous / conterminous

"Terrestrial Ecosystems of the Conterminous United States"
—US GEOLOGICAL SURVEY

Huh? Conterminous United States? Is this correct?

Yes. The temptation is to say "contiguous United States" for the lower forty-eight. But they're not contiguous, they're *conterminous*.

This is a picky distinction that is really only important if you want to show off your linguistic prowess (or get punched out as a language snob). Technically, as the *Oxford Dictionary of American Usage and Style* points out, there can't be forty-eight contiguous states. *Contiguous* means "touching, in actual contact." Obviously, all lower forty-eight states do not touch each other, so they're not contiguous. But, for example, New York and New Jersey *are* contiguous . . . even though most New Yorkers would probably rather they not be.

Contiguous comes from the Latin word *contiguus* (touching). *Conterminous*, also Latin, means "things all together enclosed within a common boundary (terminus)" and is the word we technically should be using for the lower forty-eight. But most dictionaries allow for the more casual use of *contiguous* as "neighboring" and we agree.

After all, who says "the forty-eight conterminous states"? We don't. We did a quick Google search for either contiguous or conterminous United States and found that *contiguous* was preferred two to one. Most important, many of the "conterminous" usages were from official government documents and scientific reports. But surprisingly, Google Ngram, which measures usage in printed material on a temporal basis, showed almost a tie. This shocked us. We have never met anyone who has said *conterminous*. (Maybe we need to rub shoulders more with government geographers.)

contiguous (adj): in actual contact
conterminous (adj): enclosed together within a common boundary

---

copyright / copywrite

"Baro's valse bebop, 'Survol de nuit,' surviving only as sheet music, copywritten in 1951—may never have been recorded."

—*GYPSY JAZZ: IN SEARCH OF DJANGO REINHARDT AND THE SOUL OF GYPSY SWING*

Using *copywrite* instead of the correct *copyright* is an error no self-respecting person in publishing ever makes. Of course not. (Cough, cough.)

But as you can see from the preceding example, mistakes happen even at the venerable Oxford University Press. Mixing up *copyright* and *copywriting* is most common outside of professional publishing. You can easily find examples—such as "Should I copywrite my book before or after I send it to be edited?"—posted on message boards. Here's what's wrong . . . and write . . . er, we mean *right*.

You never copywrite a book or creative work. You *copyright* it. *Copyright* is a legal right (notice "right") giving the creator of an original work the exclusive legal entitlement to his or her work, usually for a certain period of time. (After that, it's legal for anyone to use it—for example, you don't have to pay Shakespeare's heirs for the right to print his plays.) *Copywriting*—"copy" with "write"—refers to the writing of copy (aka text), most often in advertising. (And note that virtually no one says "copywrite" without the *-ing*; they say "write copy.")

Incidentally, in answer to a common question—how do I copyright what I've written?—you don't have to do anything: copyright is automatic in an original work. But it's best to put the word "copyright" or a *c* in a circle (©), along with the date of publication, and your name as the owner of all the copyright rights. Just don't write *copywrite*.

copyright (n, v): exclusive legal right to reproduce, license, etc. a literary or artistic work

crescendo

"The caterwauling horns had reached a crescendo and I turned away and cut across the lawn toward home."

—F. SCOTT FITZGERALD, *THE GREAT GATSBY*

Can something reach a crescendo? In a 2013 *New York Times* op-ed piece, a professional violist complained passionately about the misuse of this word. He pointed out (correctly) that in music a *crescendo* is the *process* of getting louder. So, no, he insisted, something can't *reach* a crescendo at all. He concluded that famous authors, like F. Scott Fitzgerald, have flagrantly misused this word.

Then the fireworks began . . . and have continued in a cacophonous crescendo. Numerous people have weighed in, passionately saying that language has changed and nowadays, yes, you can reach a crescendo; it *can* be a peak instead of a process.

So who's correct? In terms of word origins, the vehement violist is verifiably veracious. *Crescendo* comes from Italian via Latin, from the word *crescere* (to grow). *Crescendoing*, the gerund (an *-ing* noun formed from a verb), means "a growing," a process rather than an end in itself. The major dictionaries prefer this definition. In fact, the *OED* says that using *crescendo* as a peak rather than a process is just a colloquialism. It also points out rather sniffily that this usage originated in the colonies (i.e., in the United States where they speak weird English). But *American Heritage* notes that *crescendo* as "climax" is gradually becoming more acceptable: in the 1980s, 55 percent of their usage panel rejected it; now 55 percent accept it. Put one of us in the minority camp as this switch is not music to his ears.

crescendo (n, v): increase gradually in loudness or intensity

SOMETHING STINKS: STINK/STANK/STUNK
AND OTHER STRONG VERBS MADE WEAK

Irregular verbs in English such as "to stink" or "to sing" are called strong verbs, in which the past tense is formed not with an -ed but with a vowel change. "We sing the song and it stinks" becomes "We sang the song and it stank," not "We singed the song and it stinked." But many people seem to get confused when it comes to picking the right vowel. And it, well, stinks.

Speaking of things that stink, there is a section on book lovers' website GoodReads entitled "Popular They Stunk Books" where people can list books that they think stank, not stunk. And don't get us started on the film title *Honey, I Shrunk the Kids*, which makes us shrink back in horror and revulsion since, honey, he actually shrank the kids.

How do these verbs work? It all depends on when the singing, the stinking, or the shrinking happened. It should be "sang," "stank," or "shrank" when it's in the simple past tense—when it's something that happened in the past. It should be "sung," "stunk," or "shrunk" when it's in the past perfect—when you need a helping verb like "had" with the verb to convey that it happened before or during something else: "I shrank the kids yesterday. Yes, I had shrunk them before they shot the movie."

It sounds a little confusing, but it really isn't. When in doubt, just remember the words from the song in *How the Grinch Stole Christmas* ("stink, stank, stunk"). Most of the time. (See "swing," below.)

Here are a few examples:

PRESENT TENSE	SIMPLE PAST TENSE	PAST PERFECT TENSE
begin	began	begun
drink	drank	drunk
shrink	shrank	shrunk
sing	sang	sung
stink	stank	stunk
swing	swung	swung

decimate

"A 1,200-Pound Pumpkin Completely Decimated a Truck, Just for Fun"

—HEADLINE, MASHABLE

Was Mashable wrong to use "decimated"? Not really, yet many might say so. *Decimate* is a word that grammar purists love to expound upon. They say that *decimate* technically means "to kill or destroy only every tenth person or thing," so "completely decimated" is completely wrong.

Or is it? *Decimate* supposedly comes directly from the Roman Legion practice of killing one out of every ten soldiers as punishment for mutiny or other crimes. But some experts say the word didn't come from Rome but from the Medieval Latin word *decimatus*, meaning "to tithe"—or pay a tax of a tenth (ten in Latin is *decem*). Then, in a later backward formation, historians used it to describe the Roman punishment. But it's still about a tenth, right? Here, too, there's some ambiguity. The *OED* has numerous examples going back to the 1600s of *decimate* meaning "to devastate, to reduce something drastically by far more than a tenth." True, this definition is only listed third after the two tenth-related ones.

More to the point, languages change, and *decimate* is today frequently used to mean "devastate," regardless of the controversy of its origins. After all, *silly* used to mean "deserving of pity"—not so today. And anyway, who needs a word to describe one-tenth of something destroyed? When writer Ben Lucian Burman was asked if he used *decimate* to literally mean the destruction of a tenth, he replied, "Good heavens, no. How fussy can you get?"

decimate (v): to destroy or devastate

definitive / definite

> "We're starting to get more definitive. I think probably after that second Delmarva appearance, we'll get a real definitive idea if that all goes well."
>
> —ORIOLES PITCHER ZACH BRITTON, QUOTED IN THE *BALTIMORE SUN*

We've got a pretty definite idea that's not what he meant to say. (You see what we did there, right?) Yes, *definitive* doesn't mean definite, even though it looks a lot like it. They are similar, they are related, but they are not the same. Definitely not. And that's definitive. (Deftly done, no? Um, perhaps we shouldn't ask.)

To put it as briefly and basically as possible, *definite* means "precise, clearly defined." *Definitive* means "authoritatively conclusive." While both words are based on the concept of something being defined, something definitive goes a step further than something merely definite.

Etymologically speaking, they are also related yet different. Both stem from *define*, but *definite* comes from the Middle English *diffinite*, from the Latin *definitus*, meaning "defined, bounded, precise." *Definitive* comes from the French *definitif*, via the Latin *definitivus*, meaning "explanatory or definitive," which is what it means. Its first appearance in print was in the late 1300s in Chaucer's "The Physician's Tale" of his *Canterbury Tales* ("The juge answerde, "Of this, in his absence, I may nat yeve diffynytyf sentence") and its meaning hasn't changed since then.

Finally, there's the word "definate" . . . er, actually, no, there's not. That's just a misspelling that, sadly, crops up more often than one might think. Type it into Google, and you'll see hundreds of thousands of examples. Our favorite was the subject of a post

on Yahoo Answers: "What's the proper spelling for 'definate'?"
Sigh. You can't make these things up.

definitive (adj): authoritatively conclusive
definite (adj): clearly defined, certain

---

deprecate / depreciate

"Those who profess to favor freedom, yet deprecate agitation, are men who want crops without plowing up the ground."

—FREDERICK DOUGLASS, BLACKPAST.ORG

"Those who profess to favor freedom, yet depreciate agitation, are men who want crops without plowing up the ground."

—FREDERICK DOUGLASS, *FREEDOM ON MY MIND*

Did the eloquent Douglass say *deprecate* or *depreciate*? (Our answer at the end.)

Deprecate and *depreciate* started out as two words with two different basic meanings, which have gradually gotten closer. The basic meaning of *depreciate* was (and is) "to lessen in value," as in "The dollar has depreciated against the Euro." It comes from an old Latin word that had *pretium* (price) in it, so using it in a financial sense makes sense. (Yes, we thought of writing "cents.") *Deprecate*'s basic meaning was "to express disapproval of someone or something." It originally involved praying—the old Latin root word *deprecare* meant "to fend or ward off (a disaster) by prayer."

Two different words, one with money in it and one with prayer. So where's the confusion? Well, although many purists don't like it, *depreciate* has gradually come to also mean d*eprecate*. Think about it: if you depreciate or lessen something's value, you're probably also expressing disapproval of it; in fact, you're deprecating it.

Deprecate is now rare in English except for two major uses: (1) in "self-deprecating," as in "He has a wonderful self-deprecating sense of humor" and (2) in the computer industry to mean "a command or feature in a computer language that's obsolete but still supported." *Depreciate* has taken most of *deprecate*'s jobs overall, even in "self-depreciating humor." We're not happy about it—we think it depreciates the language.

[Answer: Did Douglass say *deprecate* or *depreciate*? There's no definitive answer. Both words appear in different compilations of his work. But the earliest published works have *deprecate*.]

deprecate (v): (rare) to express disapproval
depreciate (v): to lower in value or price

---

dichotomy / discrepancy / disparity

"Second, we replace the common dichotomy between compliance and noncompliance with a three-way dichotomy between three aspects of behavior: performance, compliance, and evasion."

—"BEHAVIORAL EQUITY"

Dichotomy is often mistaken to simply mean "difference" or, more commonly, *discrepancy* or *disparity*, but it actually refers to *two* things that are different. There is technically no such thing as a "three-way dichotomy." So there's a dichotomy between the example above and linguistic correctness. (Incidentally, a three-way distinction is called a *trichotomy* . . . as for four-way distinctions, well, fuggetaboudit!)

Appropriately, there are two very important things to remember when using *dichotomy*. First, *dichotomy* is about two things *only*. It comes from the ancient Greek *dikho* (in two) and *-tomy* (cutting), literally cutting in half. (There are many cutting *-tomy* words in English from the Greek, like appendectomy.) Second, it's a division of two very different things or ideas into two mutually *exclusive* parts: love and hate, war and peace, heaven and hell.

As for *discrepancy* and *disparity*, the words that are often confused with *dichotomy*, *discrepancy* is a softer word, meaning "a difference between two related or similar things," as in "There's a discrepancy between what you said you made and your reported income to the IRS." (Not that we're insinuating anything about your tax return. . . .) *Disparity* is when there is a large difference and the IRS puts you in jail for tax fraud.

If we want to muddy the waters, we could argue that there's really no such thing as a dichotomy since there are usually more than two aspects to something. Win or lose—but what about a tie? Love and hate—and indifference. So is every dichotomy actually a false dichotomy? We're (appropriately) of two minds about this.

dichotomy (n): division into two mutually exclusive different parts
discrepancy (n): difference between two or more related or similar things
disparity (n): also a difference between things, usually larger

discomfit / discomfort

> "Data confirms that time and again, during bouts of dropping
> share prices, most investors eventually just want to make the
> discomfit go away."
>
> —*FORBES*

This sentence makes us feel a bit, should we say, uncomfitable?
(No, we shouldn't.) We think the writer meant to use *discomfort*
since *discomfit* is almost solely used as a verb. (There is a very rare
usage of *discomfit* as a noun, meaning "dejection or perplexity,"
but it is, yes, very rarely used.)

The two words sound very similar and mean similar things, but
their backgrounds and initial meanings were different. *Discomfit*
first appeared in the eleventh century from the Old French
desconfit (defeated or vanquished). Over the years, it weakened
to mean "to thwart or frustrate." Nowadays, it usually means "to
make uncomfortable or uneasy," something linguists theorize
came about because people confused *discomfit* and *discomfort*.
Discomfit is also used to mean "to perplex or embarrass." But
being perplexed or embarrassed can make one uncomfortable,
right? So there's that overlap with *discomfort* again.

Discomfort is actually a newer word than *discomfit*, coming
onto the scene in the fourteenth century from the Old French
desconforter (to make uncomfortable). It initially meant "to
discourage," but nowadays is most often used as a noun meaning
"slight pain or embarrassment." It can be used as a verb (but
rarely is), meaning "to cause someone to feel uncomfortable,
distressed," which is a lot like *discomfit*, isn't it?

So there you have it: two words from different roots but with very similar meanings. And while you can use *discomfort* as both a noun and a verb, it's best to use its near-twin *discomfit* as a verb only. To do otherwise could cause you . . . oh, never mind.

discomfit (v): to make uncomfortable, uneasy
discomfort (n): slight pain or distress; (v): to distress

discreet / discrete

"Fashion designers offer discrete ways for women to carry firearms."

—*CHATTANOOGA* [TN] *TIMES FREE PRESS*

We would like to discreetly point out that there are discrete meanings for *discreet* and *discrete*. They are not the same word with a slightly different spelling. *Discreet* means "capable of keeping secrets" or "unobtrusive" while *discrete* means "separate or distinct." Both are offspring of the same Latin word, *discretus* (separate, distinct, like the current *discrete*), but they evolved to become very distinct words.

Discreet came from the Middle French *discret* and *discrète* (prudent) and by the fourteenth century meant "able to keep secrets." *Discrete* stayed the same as the Latin, but actually wasn't used that widely until the sixteenth century and then chiefly in subjects like science and music that commonly used Latin and Latinized words. Some linguists speculate that the two words were initially interchangeable. But over time, they became quite distinct, discrete if you will (or if you won't). By the eighteenth century, dictionaries had them defined as they currently are, with *discrete* meaning "separate" (and primarily used in scholastic or scientific forums) and *discreet* meaning, well, "discreet."

But many people nowadays don't seem to know the difference, thinking that *discrete* is just another way of spelling *discreet*. This leads to usages that conjure up fascinating images like this one from a bridal site: "The bodice with a mermaid neckline blends into the back through a discrete short sleeve on the shoulder." On the plus side, we haven't seen any reference to classic film *The Discrete Charm of the Bourgeoisie*. Yet.

discreet (adj): able to keep secrets, unobtrusive
discrete (adj): separate or distinct

disinterested / uninterested

"Kylie Jenner Seems So Disinterested in Blake Lively and Ryan Reynolds at the Met Gala"

—HEADLINE, ENTERTAINMENT TONIGHT ONLINE

The word *disinterested* makes a lot of language nuts very interested indeed, primarily because so many people use it to mean "not interested." But *disinterested* actually means "free from bias, impartial," *not* "having a lack of interest or being indifferent." It is *uninterested* that means "lack of interest." Think about it. We use *uninteresting* to describe something that doesn't grab us, but not *disinteresting*. So *disinterested* clearly doesn't mean "uninterested." Right?

Well, there's a catch. (Of course. This is the English language, after all!) *Disinterested* is so widely used nowadays to mean "uninterested" that dictionaries now include "uninterested" as a definition for it. (The Oxford English Corpus found that this "incorrect" meaning of *disinterested* accounted for about 25 percent of all citations.)

There is actually historical precedent for this so-called new meaning of *disinterested*. In its first recorded usage (per the *OED*) back in 1631 by poet John Donne in his "Biathanatos," an essay on suicide, it is used to mean, yes, "uninterested." ("If there be cases, wherein the party is disinterested . . . it may be lawful.") The current "free from bias" meaning didn't appear until 1659.

The two disparate meanings actually happily coexisted until the eighteenth century, when disinterested-as-uninterested faded out, leaving just disinterested-as-impartial. But in the twentieth century, the loose usage emerged and we wound up where we are today: with many people and institutions using *disinterested* to mean *uninterested*, while being corrected by definitely *not* disinterested sticklers who insist on the distinction. (We admit, we fall in the latter camp.)

disinterested (adj): unbiased
uninterested (adj): lacking interest

---

economic / economical

"Inauguration . . . Is Trump Inheriting an Economical Crisis?"

—LOFTUS WEALTH STRATEGIES, "FINANCIAL PLANNING AND WEALTH MANAGEMENT FOR SELECT INDIVIDUALS"

No, Trump inherited an *economic* crisis. (Or didn't. We're not economists, so we can't answer the question.) What we do know is that *economic* refers to the economy in general, whereas *economical* refers to people being thrifty or avoiding waste. So an "economical crisis" sounds a little weird—unless you're talking about a "crisis in thriftiness," which also, when you think about it, sounds a little weird. But it's easy to see how the two words are confused since they're both adjectives derived from *economy*.

According to dictionaries such as *Merriam-Webster's*, you should only use *economical* when you're referring to thrift or savings. (*Webster's* includes this rather macabre example of correct usage from the *Seattle Times*: "Corpse hotels are more economical than large funeral homes.") Use *economic* for virtually everything else. (So this would be correct: "Are economical corpse hotels signs of an economic death spiral in the stock market?" No, let's not go there.)

Incorrectly substituting *economical* for *economic* is not particularly unusual, and it's not a major crime against the English language. It's easy from context to see what the writer is talking about. But why do it? In doing searches for *economical* incorrectly pinch-hitting for *economic*, we found that almost always the substitution was done by foreign-language speakers writing in English. We found examples from Portugal, Italy, Indonesia, Spain, and Germany, among others. And these weren't from uneducated writers, but were usually from authors of complicated academic papers. But why not be economical in our use of English and not wastefully use incorrect words?

economic (adj): pertaining to the economy or to economics
economical (adj): frugal, money-saving

elicit / illicit

"Evidence based policy for elicit drugs"

—*BRITISH MEDICAL JOURNAL*

In the very next issue, the *British Medical Journal* ran this correction: "An editorial error late in the production of this editorial by Evan Wood . . . led to a particularly egregious typo in the title. This should, of course, be 'Evidence based policy for illicit drugs.' Ouch."

To ease the pain a bit, it's an easy error to make—*elicit* and *illicit* sound almost alike although they're far apart in meaning.

Elicit is a verb, meaning "to draw out or call forth a response, information, or reaction." *Illicit* is an adjective, meaning "unlawful," or "against societal norms or morality." *Illicit* comes from the Latin *in-* (here used as a negative) and *licere* (to be allowed), so the combo means "not allowed" (the *n* from *in-* was dropped). *Elicit* comes from the Latin *ex-* (out) and *lacere* (to entice, inveigle; the *x* in *ex-* was dropped), so the meaning is "to draw out."

Two different words with very different meanings. Fortunately, according to the *Columbia Journalism Review* (*CJR*), confusing the two words has become increasingly less common—in their words, "it's hard to 'elicit' an 'illicit' usage, nowadays." Or is it? Doing a quick Google search, we found a radio news article about "a song [that] even illicited a response from the White House today," and many, many references to "elicit drugs." You might say we elicited many illicit usages. Sorry, *CJR*!

elicit (v): to draw out a response, reaction, information
illicit (adj): unlawful

elide

> "Yet, Tories subliminally elide these changes with the collapse of civilisation as we know it."
>
> —*THE GUARDIAN*, US EDITION

Elide means "to omit," not "to conflate," nor, more colloquially, "to mush together," yet it is getting more and more common to use it in the "mush together" way.

Elide entered English in the 1590s as a legal term first meaning "to annihilate evidence," then "to annul," evolving from the Latin *elidere* (to crush out). Over time, its meaning extended to outside the legal field, and came to be used to mean to strike out, suppress, or simply omit something. From 1796 on, it also came to be used in a linguistic sense, meaning "to omit a sound or syllable of a word." Since the omission is sometimes described as a slurring, this may be one of the reasons people seem to think *elide* means to slide over or blur rather than omit.

And it is this that is causing debate in language circles. Grammar sticklers hold that, when used outside of the grammar sense, *elide* should mean "omit," period, end of discussion. But other language people say that there is nothing wrong with the evolution of *elide* to mean "blurring," that it actually fills a need in the English language.

Columnist Guy Keleny of the [United Kingdom] *Independent* put it very bluntly: "We do have a use for a verb that means 'to smear things together. . . .' It looks as if we are deciding to use 'elide' in that role. To stand in the way would be pedantry."

And there you have it.

elide (v): to omit

emigrate / immigrate

"It was precisely for reasons such as what happened with the Solowheel that Chen emigrated to the United States in 1986."
—FORBES

That example is only 1 of 920,000 wrong uses of *emigrate* we found in a Google search. (Who knows how many we would have found if we had used Bing? Oh, never mind.)

It all depends on whether you're talking about coming from or going to. To *emigrate* is the "coming from" word—it means "to leave your country or home." *Immigrate* is the "going to" verb—it means "to move to a new country or place." The United States calls itself a nation of immigrants because most people (or their parents or grandparents, etc.) came from somewhere else. They emigrated from the rest of the world and immigrated to the United States (not to the advantage of the indigenous people already living there who weren't then in the position of being able to set immigration quotas).

One confusing point: Often immigrants to a foreign land who are now living there are also referred to as *emigres*, i.e., people who emigrated and became immigrants. The easiest way to remember the differences is to note that *immigrate* begins with *i* and so does *in*. *Emigrate* begins with *e* and so does *exit*. (And sure enough, *emigrate* comes from the Latin *ex-* (out of; it lost the *x* part in English) and *migrare* (to migrate)—and you can guess that the *imm* in *immigrate* comes from the Latin *in*; the *n* sound got assimilated into *m*.

So let's now emigrate from this page on to a new topic.

emigrate (v): to leave your country or home for another
immigrate (v): to move to a new country or home from another

eminent / immanent / imminent

"Is War Eminent on the Korean Peninsula?"

—HEADLINE, AMERICAN URBAN RADIO NETWORK WEBSITE

"US Confusion over Definition of 'Immanent Threat' Enables Abuse of Executive Power"

—THE BLAZE NETWORK

Blame it on heinous homophony. In both cases, the word should have been the like-sounding *imminent* instead of *eminent* or *immanent*. *Imminent* means "about to happen," which is what the writers were trying to say. Now we'll imminently (in a minutely?) give you the distinctions.

Immanent is a fancy, less common word meaning "existing within or inherent." It is particularly bandied about in theology, as in ". . . the World is immanent in God, as that God is immanent in the World."

Eminent means "distinguished or standing out," as in "The eminent theologian sees divine immanence in the world." Some linguists surmise that both *imminent* and *eminent* derive from the same Latin root word *mons* (mountain). This makes sense. Eminent and especially preeminent people (*eminent* with the prefix *pre-,* meaning "before or super eminent") jut out from the crowd, and *imminent* things loom before us as we near them.

And now here's a rare word for the connoisseur: *immanentize*. It's usually used with *eschaton* (end of the world), meaning "to bring about the final state of heaven on Earth," as in this from the *Orange County* [CA] *Register*, with a helpful definition for virtually all of us who didn't know the word: ". . . they brought

[President Obama] one step closer to the moment when he could ascend to the nation's highest office and immanentize the eschaton (or, create heaven on Earth)." One perplexing question: If you've got to define the word you've used, why use it at all? Just asking.

eminent (adj): distinguished
immanent (adj): existing within or inherent
imminent (adj): about to happen

---

enervated

"Drohan, her initial shift from near-catatonia to mega-smiling politesse reaching hilariously enervated levels—'Great! Great-great!'—is a comic find."

—*LOS ANGELES TIMES*

The *Los Angeles Times* praised a comic performance as "*enervated*," which means "tired and exhausted." Not to criticize critics, but we will take a not-so-bold stand and say we think they meant to say "energized" or "invigorating."

Thinking that *enervated* means its opposite is an exceedingly common mistake. Back in 1934, psychometrician Johnson O'Connor (who had a penchant for collecting data on virtually everything vocabulary-related) wrote that precisely 52 percent of college graduates he surveyed were making the same mistake.

Enervate comes from the Late Latin noun *enervatio,* a combination of two words—*ex-* (out of) and *nervus* (sinew, or nerve), literally meaning "to cut the sinews." It was commonly used in this literal sense as late as the 1700s (the *Chambers Encyclopedia of 1728* rather bizarrely talks about enervating horse's nerves to make their heads small), as well as in the sense of a more general weakening. After the 1700s, probably because people stopped enervating animals, this latter definition became the one used.

Nowadays when we see or hear the word *enervated*, we don't even vaguely or subliminally think of cutting nerves or sinews. Instead, we more probably visualize a similar-sounding word—*energized*—and figure *enervated* is just a fancy way of saying that. People talk and write about "brisk, enervating showers" or "exciting, enervating concerts" all the time. There's absolutely no need to delve further and talk about a recent online ad that happily promised impotent men a treatment to totally enervate their penises. Ouch!

enervated/enervating (adj): tired, tiring

---

enormity / enormous

"Crowd sizes for the March for Life are impossible to ascertain with certainty, in part because of the enormity of the crowds. . . ."
—*NATIONAL REVIEW*

The writer presumably thought the enormity of the crowds was a good thing. If so, he made a (relatively) enormous mistake.

Enormity often does mean "large"—but in a bad sense, as in "the enormity of crimes committed by the evil dictator." It also means plain old "bad or wicked." It isn't simply a more euphonious way of expressing enormousness. Nowadays, the vocabularily liberal *Merriam-Webster's* includes a positive usage, but only as a grudging third definition. Meanwhile, the more conservative *OED* is sticking with only the negative definition, although they do add that *enormity* can mean "large in a humorous sense," as in this from an 1826 book: "This waxen enormity [sc. an enormous taper] was lighted." (Note: The humor eludes us.) It's easy to understand the confusion. Both *enormous* and *enormity* are derived from the Latin *ex-* (out of) and *norma* (rules, norms), "out of normal bounds." Both words bounded into English with a negative sense. Sometime in the 1500s, *enormous* also got a more positive general meaning of "huge or big," while *enormity* retained its meaning as "an *excess* of something, a transgression, out of bounds behavior," i.e., bad big.

So what to do with *enormity*? We say avoid using it for *enormous* in the positive sense, i.e., good or neutral big. Some pundits say replace *enormity* with *enormousness*, but that sounds clunky to us. Immensity? Vastness? Bigness? Fortunately, English is a language rich in synonyms. Some might say it has an enormity of synonyms, but we wouldn't.

enormity (n): most commonly, wickedness or an evil act
enormous (adj): huge, immense

---

epicenter

"The [Chateau de Lafayette] inn promotes itself as being at the epicenter of a circle of state parks and nearby attractions, although most are found in neighboring counties."

—VISITFLORIDA WEBSITE, ON THE LAFAYETTE INN, LAFAYETTE, FLORIDA

Visualize an inn floating high above the ground like a balloon while far below a ring of Florida state parks and nearby attractions encircles the inn's position and you've got what the example above is telling us, according to the preferred definition of *epicenter*.

We're guessing the Chateau de Lafayette's location is on the more mundane ground level. Herein lies the problem with *epicenter*. It literally means "the point *above* the center." It's commonly used by geologists in earthquake terminology to mean the point on the earth's surface over the subterranean center of an earthquake. It comes from the ancient Greek, combining *epi-* (on, on top of) and *kentron* (center).

Okay. Now here's where we get targeted as language pedants. *Epicenter* is sometimes also used figuratively to mean the center of activity, or even simply the center, as in "the epicenter of world finance." So you could argue quite convincingly that the Visitflorida website is correct. Moreover, many accomplished writers use it, like James Joyce, who used it geographically in his classic novel *Ulysses*: "The epicentre seems to have been that part of the metropolis that constitutes the Inn's Quay ward and parish of Saint Michans." (We assume that he wasn't talking about airborne wards and parishes.) But we've always preferred Hemingway, and we think he would have said, "Why use epicenter to figuratively mean center when you can use center to literally mean center?" And in fewer letters, too.

epicenter (n): the point on the earth's surface above the underground center of an earthquake

epitaph / epithet

"A landlord used racial epitaphs to demean a tenant."

—ANTI-DEFAMATION LEAGUE WEBSITE

Many people call *epithets* "*epitaphs*." Maybe it's because *epithet* isn't a euphonious word—the *epith* in *epithet* sounds like a lisp and the tongue stumbles. (The only other common *epith* word in English is *epithelial*.) *Epitaph* sounds better.

Unfortunately for euphony, you can't substitute one for the other. An *epithet* is a description of a person or thing using certain qualities or characteristics they possess (or you think they possess). Although *epithets* aren't necessarily negative, they often are. We're all unfortunately familiar with many racial or religious ones that should die away. And speaking of dying, when someone is writing (usually on a tombstone) or saying words in memory of someone, that's an *epitaph*.

Epitaph comes from the ancient Greek *epitaphion*, with *epi-* (over) and *taphion* (tomb), clearly indicating the ancient meaning—"a memorial oration over a tomb." The meaning hasn't changed much since then. *Epithet* comes from ancient Greek as well, although its derivation isn't certain. The Greeks used the word as we do, but more often positively. Epithets are all over Greek literature, particularly Homer, as in his beautiful epithets like "rosy-fingered" dawn and "bright-eyed" goddess Athene. The Greeks also had other *epi-* literary words, like *epithalamium*—a lyric ode to newlyweds, in use in English as late as the 1800s—and *epicedium*—a funeral ode, used by the ancient Greeks and classically minded British. We even found an epicedium in a most unlikely place, a novel by suspense writer

Dean Koontz: "Outside, the wind and rain sang an epicedium for the dead."

epitaph (n): inscription on a tomb or grave in honor of the deceased
epithet (n): description of a person's attributes or qualities, usually
  negative

---

eponymous

"His first record, the eponymous *Bob Dylan*, was filled with original songs alongside traditional songs. . . ."
—*WASHINGTON POST*

Here's another one for grammar purists. (And we will admit at the outset that we consider this a "resistance is futile" situation.) We speak of *eponymous*—a smart-sounding adjective based on the smart-sounding noun *eponym* that has skyrocketed in use since about 1980.

An *eponym* is something or someone that gives its name to something else. So *eponymous* is technically used to describe the name *giver*, not the name receiver. In the example above, then, it actually should be "His first record, *Bob Dylan*, named after the eponymous musician." Clunky, yes, but correct. But lately *eponymous* is more widely used to describe the name *receiver* rather than the traditional giver. Thus we see frequent references to "Joe's eponymous business" or "Dylan's eponymous album." This, of course, rankles the stricter grammarians among us.

While *eponymous* has become more widely used over time— it shows up in published works about six times more now than it did in the 1800s—it's also more loosely used. A quick Google search found it used more often in the nontraditional sense than the traditional. So what to do?

Well, there's a way to avoid the whole kerfuffle, especially since often *eponymous* is used as a furbelow, an "I'm smart!" descriptor. So we're with *New York Times* columnist Philip Corbet when he said, "Often, there's a way to say what we mean without using 'eponymous' at all. So let's use it sparingly, and wisely." Can we call that the *eponymous* Corbet Rule? Nah.

eponymous (adj): giving its/their name to something

---

facetious / sarcastic

"'Please try Obamacare today,' Seinfeld says to the camera with a facetious smile."

—MSNBC.COM

In reading this, we're not smiling facetiously, chiefly because there is no such thing as a facetious smile. *Facetious* refers to words, not actions. What you say is facetious, but the accompanying smile isn't.

Using *facetious* to describe an action is only one common mistake people make when using the word. They also often use it interchangeably with *sarcastic*, but while similar in meaning, the words are also distinct.

At its broadest, *facetious* means "amusing, something not intended to be taken seriously." But many dictionaries take it one step further, noting that it is often deliberately inappropriate, flippant. This is why it's so often confused with *sarcastic*.

Facetious came to English in about 1590, directly from the French *facétieux*, from the Latin *facetiae* (jests), which came from *facetus* (witty, elegant). *Sarcastic* came from the Greek *sarkasmos*, literally "to strip the flesh from a piece of meat." And therein lies the difference. A facetious remark is jocular, more gentle; a sarcastic one is cutting, sneering.

(As a total side note: *facetious* is one of very few words in English that have all five vowels in order. The others are *abstemious*, and the much rarer *abstentious*, *achelious*, *anemious*, *annelidous*, and *caesious*. And as a note even further on the side: In the reading world, the plural noun *facetiae* has been used not only to refer to a collection of jokes, but also, more slyly, as a euphemism for erotica or pornography.)

facetious (adj): flippant, amusing in an inappropriate way
sarcastic (adj): caustically mocking or contemptuous

factoid

"On Monday, Kensington Palace released an all-important teaser of a factoid about the upcoming ceremony, one that's sure to please a legion of royals fans. . . ."

—*TIME*

Until very recently (okay, until we began researching this book), we assumed, like many others, that a factoid was a little fact, a snippet of information, something either brief or trivial and that was that. As you probably have guessed, that wasn't that at all.

When you look at the word itself, you can see its original meaning. The suffix *-oid* means "resembling, but not the same." Think of planetoids or humanoids. So when you add the *-oid* to *fact*, you get something that is similar to but not the same as a fact. Writer Norman Mailer coined the term in 1973 in *Marilyn*, his biography of Marilyn Monroe, where he defined it as "facts which have no existence before appearing in a magazine or newspaper, creations which are not so much lies as a product to manipulate emotion in the Silent Majority." Nothing about a mini-fact there at all.

But no matter what Mailer intended, over time *factoid* became used more and more often to mean "brief fact," mainly due to the media like CNN Headline News, which was one of the prime users of "factoid as factlet"—putting brief facts on the screen with the header "factoid." Now dictionaries have succumbed to the inevitable and have the "brief news item" as their primary definition of factoid . . . just the way we've always used it (and will continue to use it) anyway.

factoid (n): originally, something similar to a fact, now also a brief or trivial fact

farther / further

"But according to small business investor and turnaround king Marcus Lemonis, that couldn't be farther from the truth."

—CNBC.COM

Let's cut to the chase before we go any farther . . . or further: (1) Which one is it? (2) Furthermore (sorry), does it matter? The short answers: (1) In the case of the phrase "further from the truth," *further* is preferred. (2) It depends.

The basic rule of thumb you often hear, promoted by such grammar authorities as the *AP Stylebook*, is that *farther* is for physical distances ("That is farther away") and *further* for figurative distances ("That couldn't be further from the truth!"). The handy mnemonic for this: *Farther* has "far" in it, and far relates to actual distance, so when it's real distance, it's *farther*, not *further*.

But the question remains: is this distinction necessary or are we going further (figurative distance!) with correctness than we need to? After all, *farther* and *further* were used interchangeably for centuries. In fact, *farther* entered the language in the fifteenth century as a variation of the older *further*. The distinction between *farther* and *further* didn't come about until the mid-nineteenth century, a creation of American grammarians. (The further/farther dilemma doesn't arise in other English-speaking countries, especially since *farther* is not widely used.)

We fall into the "it doesn't really matter" camp and see no reason why you can't use either one whenever you please. But, that said, you might run across some backlash. Even the very descriptive *Merriam-Webster's* dictionary notes that, while they can be used interchangeably when actual distance isn't involved, *further* is the preferred choice in American English.

farther (adj, adv): greater physical distance
further (adj, adv): greater figurative distance

foment / ferment

"Rising out of the foment of the mid-19th century, the 'Ring' is often seen as a work with strong Marxist overtones."

—THE ECONOMIST

There seems to be a trend lately of using *foment* as a noun where *fomentation* or *ferment* would do just fine. And, frankly, we think this is fomenting trouble.

Foment is a transitive verb meaning "to incite or stir up." As such, it is used when there is an object that is being stirred up, usually something negative like trouble or war. It was used as a noun in the past, but this form is now rare or obsolete. The *OED* listing for the noun *foment* gives examples that end in 1892.

So why, several centuries later, is foment-as-noun gaining in popularity? It is probably the old "it sounds so much like another word, let's use it where we'd use that" issue.

In this case, the other word is *ferment*. As a verb it means "to undergo fermentation," of course, but also figuratively "to rouse, incite, or excite." And as a noun, it refers to the excitement or agitation that has been roused. So people are slipping *foment* in for *ferment*, thinking they're interchangeable. They're not, of course. While it's a new trend now, it had been an issue in the past as well. The third definition for the noun *foment* in the *OED* is "confused with ferment," with an example from 1793 when none other than Thomas Jefferson used it incorrectly in his *Writings:* "Should the present foment in Europe not produce republics everywhere."

ferment (v): to undergo fermentation, to stir up; (n): something stirred up
foment (v): to incite, stir up

firmament

> "This is not as simple as it sounds, however, as every time the ball comes into contact with the firmament, play is stopped."
>
> —MEAN MACHINES ARCHIVE, HISTORICAL GAMES REVIEW OF JOHN MADDEN FOOTBALL COMPUTER GAME

Footballs can't hit the firmament, unless Mean Machines players are describing an ancient biblical computer football game, which, we suspect, Old Testament types never played.

More to the point, *firmament* is *not* the ground, although a surprisingly large number of people think it is. *Firmament* is *"above* the ground, the expanse of the sky above." Metaphorically, it's also used to denote a collection of people, usually in a positive sense, as in "the glittering firmament of stars at the Oscars."

Firmament comes from the Latin *firmamentum* (a prop or support), which in turn comes from the Latin *firmus* (firm). It came to mean the vault or expanse of the sky via the Latin translation of the biblical Hebrew word *raqia* derived from *raqq∂'*, "to beat or spread out," as in hammering a lump of metal, and spreading or expanding it to make a bowl or dish. This leads to a continuing and astonishingly vicious argument among certain biblically oriented people: did the ancient Israelites believe that the firmament or sky above was hard like a literal inverted bowl? Most say yes, but others argue that *raqia* meant "expanse" and said nothing at all regarding the firmness of the sky. The argument for and against the early belief in a solid sky can get heated, enough to melt a putatively firm firmament. For our purposes, who cares? The *firmament* is the great expanse of the sky, and whether firm or not, let's look upward and use the word correctly.

firmament (n): the vault or expanse of sky, also can be used metaphorically

---

flair / flare

"Whether or not it works as art, Famous has reinforced [Kanye] West's reputation as a skillful appropriator with a flare for controversy."

—*THE GUARDIAN*, US EDITION

Whatever you may think of Kanye, there's one thing certain: he might be a skillful appropriator, but he definitely doesn't have "a flare for controversy." That's because there is no such thing. The *Guardian* has fallen into a homonym trap and should have used *flair*.

Flare—used as both a noun or a verb—is connected with fire, either literally ("the candle flared") or figuratively ("the tempers flared"), or means something spreading out ("the jeans flared"). No one is quite sure where it came from, just that it entered the English language in the mid-1500s and *might* have come from Scandinavian or Dutch.

Flair, on the other hand, has a definite history. While currently most often used to mean "a special aptitude or ability," it initially meant "an odor." The word comes from the Old French *flairier* (to smell), from the Latin *flagrare* (from *fragrare*, to emit an odor—as in today's *fragrance*), and was mainly a hunting term referring to a hound's nose. By the mid-1920s, it evolved from the literal smelling something to the metaphorical, as in someone having "a nose for news," or "a flair for news." There's even a newer meaning that emerged in the 1950s—*flair* used to describe a sense of style.

Nowadays use of the wrong *flare* is increasing. When we plugged "dramatic flare" and "dramatic flair" into the Google Ngram reader, we found that, while the correct *flair* is still beating out the incorrect *flare*, its usage is going down while *flare* flares.

flair (n): a special aptitude or ability
flare (n): outburst of flame; (v): to burn with a flame or spread out

flammable / inflammable

"Inflammable means flammable? What a country!"
—DR. NICK RIVERA, *THE SIMPSONS*

Thanks, Dr. Nick! Right, there's no difference between *flammable* and *inflammable*. Not only in the United States but everywhere they speak English. Both mean "combustible, easily set on fire." But many people don't know or forget this, and think *inflammable* means "not burnable." As the not-so-bright Woody the barman on classic television show *Cheers* says, "Boy, did I find that one out the hard way."

Unfortunately, language is not necessarily logical, and the prefix *in-* (originally Latin) can have different meanings. We most commonly use *in-* as added onto words to mean "not," as in "intolerant." So why doesn't *inflammable* mean "not burnable?" Because there are other meanings of *in-* as well. The prefix *in-* can simply mean "in," it can be used as a way of making the word more intense, as a way of making a verb transitive, as a causative, and as a sort of throw-in sound with little meaning.

In the case of *inflammable*, the *in-* came via Old French, from the Latin, and it meant "to cause something to burn." But in the 1920s, when people became concerned over the dangers of confusion, they dropped the *in-* from *inflammable*. However, we still use other *flammable*-related words with the *in-*. For example, we don't say *flammation*, we say *inflammation*. (Note: The opposite of inflammable or flammable is "not combustible" or "not flammable." That's a lot less confusing than the French for the same word—with two "ins!"—*ininflammable*. Quelle horreur!)

flammable (adj): inflammable; capable of being easily ignited and of burning quickly
inflammable (adj): flammable; easily inflamed, excited, or angered

---

flaunt / flout

"No matter the insanity of the secretaries in charge of the environment, education, energy, or other departments, none seems as willing to openly flaunt the rule of law as Trump."
—SALON

We somehow doubt that many individuals are tempted to flaunt the rules, whatever rules they may be, since *flaunt* means "to ostentatiously show off." How many rules are show off–worthy? Now *flouting*, or willfully ignoring, the rules is another story.

Flaunt and *flout* are commonly mistaken for each other. And, in fairness, it's a very easy mistake to make since *flaunt* and *flout* are paronyms—they look and sound similar. They even entered into English at about the same time. But, of course, they aren't interchangeable.

Flout first came on the scene in the 1550s, meaning "to treat with disdain," probably from the Middle English *floute*, "to play on the flute," also "to whistle or hiss derisively." *Flaunt*, "to show oneself off in flashy clothing," entered English about a decade later, but no one is quite sure what its origins are. The sense of the word that we use today, showing off or brazenly displaying, didn't come about until 1827. Both words have retained their meanings and, as you can see, there's really no crossover.

Of course, there are those who say "flaunting the rules" isn't really that bad, chiefly because so many people use it. For example, *Merriam-Webster's* cites numerous examples from contexts they say "cannot be called substandard." However, also note that if you use it, you should prepare yourself for people correcting you.

flaunt (v): to brazenly show off
flout (v): to openly disregard a rule or law

---

flounder / founder

"Nine days later, a hurricane sank the ship off of the coast of Cape Hatteras, North Carolina, all but 109 perished as the ship floundered and sank."

—ARAGO (NATIONAL POSTAL MUSEUM OF THE SMITHSONIAN INSTITUTION) WEBSITE, DESCRIPTION OF A MODEL OF THE SS *GEORGE LAW*

To flounder or to founder, that is the question. We're not talking about the tasty flatfish, but of the verbs to *flounder* and to *founder*. First, the dictionary definitions: to *flounder* is "to move aimlessly, awkwardly, or struggle to maintain position." To *founder* is "to fill with water and sink, or to fail utterly." So can ships flounder?

Most grammarians say no, although clearly many people think they can—a recent Google search turned up 4,157 ships floundering. Five times more ships foundered.

True, the words do have an overlap. The difference is severity. *Floundering* is struggling to keep position, whereas *foundering* is going one further: failing and sinking. Some say that a ship can easily flounder before it founders. But that's pushing things, in our opinion. (Some ambitious types have said that *floundering* as used to describe sinking ships comes from the observation of flounders flopping around on land or on deck after they've been caught. But there's no credible etymology that supports this etymological floundering.) It seems nice and shipshape to stay with ships foundering on reefs and icebergs, and forgo nautical floundering. Either word can be used with people, sports teams, and the like depending on the severity of the problem: "Yankees Continue to Flounder" (MSN.com) or "Powerless Alex biggest player in Yankees' foundering lineup" (Sportsnet). Note, however, that the Yankees kept (metaphorically) afloat throughout the season, so perhaps more correctly we should have said they only floundered, and never foundered. And we're not even Yankees fans.

flounder (v): to move aimlessly, to struggle to maintain position
founder (v): to sink after being filled with water; metaphorically, to fail or collapse

forward / foreword

"In the forward of the book, Copeland writes that there was no glam squad on the set, and she was blown away by the final photos."

—FOX NEWS ENTERTAINMENT

We never read the book in question, but we can tell you one thing: there wasn't a forward to it.

Fox has fallen headlong into the forward/foreword trap. People who should know better, including editors, journalists, and writers, mix up the two homonyms and refer to "forwards" of books when it should be "forewords." Some people even use the invented combo word *foreward*. So let's step backward to make sense of this.

Forward means, of course, "to the front, moving ahead," and comes from the Old English, combining *fore* (front) with *-ward* (direction), and is used as an adjective, adverb, or noun. *Foreword* is a noun only, from *fore* (front) and *word*, literally meaning "front word." *Foreword* is a much younger word than *forward*, first being used in print in the mid-1800s. The *OED* succinctly defines it as "a word said before something else; hence, an introduction, a preface."

Speaking of a foreword, an introduction, and a preface: what (if any) is the technical difference between them?

The foreword, says the *Chicago Manual of Style*, is usually written by someone other than the author, often someone prominent to entice readers. (We recall a book cover emblazoned with a huge "Foreword by Jerry Seinfeld," beneath which was the tiny name of the author.) The introduction, by the author, talks about the book's subject. The preface (which comes between the two) is almost always by the author and typically explains why he or she wrote the book. (Usually the principal reason, money, is left politely unsaid.)

foreword (n): a brief intro to a book
forward (adj, adv): to the front; moving ahead

fortuitous

"Perhaps it's fortuitous that Davis signed with the Chargers."
—*LOS ANGELES TIMES*

It's very common to use *fortuitous* to mean "lucky or fortunate"—which is quite *un*fortunate.

When something is *fortuitous*, it has happened by accident. It has come about by chance or, yes, fortune, but (and this is the key) not necessarily *good* fortune. There's no good or bad about something fortuitous. The word comes from the Latin *fortuitus*—a combo of *forte* (by chance), which comes from *fors* (chance), and an *-ous* (full of) suffix. So *fortuitous* literally means "full of chance, something undesigned," not fortunate. While *fortunate* is related to the root *fors*, by way of the word *fortuna*, it followed a different evolutionary path, stemming from the twelfth-century Old French *fortune*, which evolved from the Latin *fortunatus* (prosperous, lucky), from *fortunare* (to make prosperous).

Because *fortuitous* is so often misused to mean a lucky accident, there is some pushback saying it is fine used as such. It's the "informal" meaning, as some dictionaries put it. But "informal," in this case, is pretty much a euphemism

for "wrong," as far as we're concerned. And we're not alone.
Harvard linguist Steven Pinker includes *fortuitous* on his list of
the most commonly misused words in the English language—to
which we say it is indeed fortunate (not fortuitous) to be among
such illustrious company.

fortuitous (adj): happened by chance or accident

from whence / whence

"The Ring was made in the fires of Mount Doom; only there can
it be unmade. It must be taken deep into Mordor and cast back
into the fiery chasm from whence it came."

—ELROND, IN THE FILM *THE LORD OF THE RINGS:
THE FELLOWSHIP OF THE RING*

Even half-elven leaders like Elrond make mistakes. *Whence*
means "from where" or "from what place." Notice the "from"
in the definition. So Elrond's "from whence" means "from from
where," obviously a bit redundant—and technically more than a
bit wrong.

That said, for many English speakers, saying or writing
"whence you came" begs for the preposition "from." It just
sounds better. The *Urban Dictionary* disagrees, stating that
if you use "from" with "whence" "you are a dick." Well, there
have been many such "dicks" dating all the way back to the
thirteenth century.

A very thorough study found "from whence" was used by such
great writers as Shakespeare, Defoe, Dickens, Dryden, Gibbon,
and Twain. It also was used twenty-seven times in the King
James Bible (including Psalm 121:1: "I will lift up mine eyes unto

the hills, from whence cometh my help"). We'll add Hobbes and Ralph Waldo Emerson, newspapers like the *Washington Post*, political blogs like *Counterpunch*, and US presidents like JFK to the list.

So if they all did it, should we? Even though at this point *from whence* is now a (somewhat) acceptable idiom and increasingly popular—one hundred years ago "whence" was used ten times more frequently than "from whence"; the ratio today is one to one—we say why bother being wrong and being corrected? For that matter, why use the archaic-sounding *whence* at all? Say "from where" instead. And as for Elrond, his first language was Elvish, not English, so he's forgiven.

whence (adv): from where

fulsome

"Stylish Design and Fulsome Bass Makes for an Ideal Wireless Speaker"

—HEADLINE, *FORBES*

Use *fulsome* like the *Forbes* headline writer did above, and some people will think it's just fine. *Fulsome* = abundant, rich. But other people, including us, will explain that *fulsome* actually means "insincerely flattering" and the positive *fulsome* is an annoying new definition that has come about because people use it so often. Who's right? We side with us.

Back in the thirteenth century, when *fulsome* emerged in Middle English, a combo of *ful* (full) and the suffix -*some* (to a considerable degree), it meant exactly what it implied, "plentiful or abundant." By the mid-fourteenth century, it became more negative, meaning "fleshy, overfed." Then it was extended even more to mean "arousing disgust or offensive." Some linguists believe this stemmed from the concept of overeating, which can cause nausea; others point to the *ful* and say it was confused with *foul*, leading to the negative connotations. In the fifteenth century, it also came to mean "effusively praising or excessively flattering," a definition that has stuck with it to the present.

But over time, the original meaning started creeping back, and the "full" concept began taking hold, even while prescriptivists squawked. And they are still squawking. So what to do? We recommend staying out of trouble by avoiding the term altogether, since it can elicit negative connotations to some. After all, you can fulsome of the people some of the time, but. . . .

fulsome (adj): insincerely flattering, also abundant, large (not preferred)

---

grizzly / grisly

"I see the intrigue, the back-stabbing, and the grizzly horror of a good old right-wing food fight."

—HUFFINGTON POST

Stop! We can't, er, bear it! Not the concept of a food fight, but that *grizzly*. Unless there was something ursine going on, the word should be *grisly*.

This is another case of homophonic horror. The two words sound alike, so they are confused with one another even though they are spelled differently and mean entirely different things.

Something *grisly* causes horror or terror. The word comes from the Old English *grislic* (horrible or dreadful), which sprang from the Germanic word *grisan* (to shudder). Beyond that, though, no one is absolutely sure of its history. It first appeared in the 1100s and initially meant "causing extreme dread." Today's meaning is a bit watered down, used more to describe something gruesome than something ultimately terrifying.

Grizzly, on the other hand, means "gray or grayish," formed from the Old French *grisel,* which came from the word for gray, *gris*. It isn't quite as old as *grisly*, but it has been used since the late 1300s. Nowadays, while you can sometimes see the word *grizzled*, you typically don't see *grizzly* used unless referring to the North American bear (*Ursus arctos horriblis*, "horrible bear"), which was named in 1807 by a member of the Lewis and Clark expedition. A grizzly, granted, can cause horror or terror, but isn't grisly itself.

Yet *grizzly* for *grisly* pops up quite often. So we read of grizzly crime scenes (involving no bears) or, our favorite, grizzly zombies, which we were sorry to read were not zombified bears at all, but your run-of-the-mill human zombie.

grisly (adj, adv): causing horror or terror
grizzly (adj): gray; (n): bear

historic / historical

"It was an historical day on Wall Street, the biggest intraday drop ever!"

—FOX BUSINESS NETWORK ANCHOR

The example above is technically correct, but that's pushing it. *Every* past day is a historical day. But only a few days are historic.

Historical merely means "based in history," so anything that happened in the past is historical and not necessarily news. Yesterday when I ate a chicken salad sandwich on rye bread—that was historical. *Historic* means "significant or famous in history," or "having a long history." Yesterday when I ate that chicken salad sandwich—no, that wasn't historic. A huge drop in the stock market, on the other hand, is big news, and that *is* historic. We're sure the Fox anchor wasn't trying to say it was just another day on the Street with the biggest intraday drop ever—she was talking about a big down day that should go down in history. (It was a probably a historic day with many *hysterical* people as well, but that's another story.)

This distinction between *historic* and *historical* is interesting because it's recent. In Shakespeare's day, you could easily use *historical* to mean *historic* and vice versa without arousing attention. In fact, you still can, especially in England. But in the USA, *Merriam-Webster's* says "modern convention" prefers to keep the words distinct. You could say that historical usage to them isn't as important as current usage, and we completely agree with *Merriam-Webster's*.

historic (adj): significant or famous in history
historical (adj): concerning or belonging in the past

home in / hone in

"Home Capital Honing In on New CEO, CFO"

—HEADLINE, TORONTO.COM

We would have been happier if it were "Hone Capital Homing In on," even though there is no Hone Capital (or so we suspect). At least that would have been grammatically correct. *Honing* means "sharpening"; there technically is no "honing in." One *homes* in.

The "home" part of the phrase is from the Old and Middle English *hamian,* which sounds like what it meant, "to establish in a home." *Homing in* appears to have been most widely used in the 1800s to refer to the ability of carrier pigeons to return to their birdly abodes. (Interested readers are directed to the 1886 issue of the *Poultry Monthly*, volume 8, p. 287, for a detailed, if somewhat overenthusiastic, discussion of homing pigeons.) By the 1920s, *homing in* was used for aircraft and missiles, which were guided to a target or destination by radio signals. From there, it came into mainstream English as a metaphor for anyone or anything focusing on or directed toward a goal.

Hone seems to have sliced its way into the phrase *homing in* and slashed out the "home" part due to its similarity. This appears to have been a late-twentieth-century phenomenon: *honing in* jumped into use in the mid-1960s; it was virtually unused before then. By the year 2000, it was used as frequently as *home in*. But leave honing to knives and lawn-mower blades and home in on the correct word.

home in (v): to move toward a target
hone: to sharpen

hopefully

"Mayor Offers $32 Million Plan to Ice Some Rats. Hopefully."

—HEADLINE, *NEW YORK TIMES*

The example above is a rare instance when the *Times* went against its own stylebook and incorrectly used *hopefully* as "it is to be hoped." Hey, it happens. We're guilty, too. It's just a technical nit-picking issue and we think we all should get over it.

According to strict usage fiends, *hopefully* should only be used as an adverb meaning "in a hopeful manner." Look at the above example and try substituting "in a hopeful manner" for *hopefully*. You'll see it doesn't work. So were the *Times* copy editors wrong?

We say no. And in fact, the *Times* itself in 2012 published an article defending the usage of *hopefully* as "to be hoped" and supporting it with a certain grammatical rationale. As with some other adverbs, including *clearly*, *certainly*, and *thankfully*, *hopefully* can function as a "sentence adverb"—modifying the entire sentence rather than just a single verb. Thankfully, this is self-evident; hopefully, you understand.

Some don't like it. Strunk and White, in their famous *The Elements of Style*, denounced it back in the 1930s in a long tirade, poet Phyllis McGinley said it was "an abomination" and (rather overdramatically) suggested lynching misusers of *hopefully*. We'll give her poetic license on that count. Many others say it's here to stay and we all had better get used to it. We agree, and hopefully you do, too.

hopefully (adv): in a hopeful manner; now also, to be hoped

A, *AE*, *I*, OR *S*?: PROBLEMATIC PLURALS IN ENGLISH WORDS INHERITED FROM LATIN AND GREEK

Plurals that come from Latin and Greek and are formed by adding an *i*, *es*, *ae*, or *a* to the ending (like alumnae or cacti) can complicate matters for otherwise verbally acute individuals. The issue: when to *s* and when to *a*—or *ae*, or *i*?

In their zeal to sound correct, some people blithely tack on an old Greek or Latin plural ending when they shouldn't. For example, when Donald Trump was talking about his TV show *The Apprentice*, he said he always enjoyed meeting all the "apprenti." (We hope he was joking, but we think he wasn't.) On the flip side, some people use the technically correct *i* or *ae* ending, but wind up sounding ridiculously pedantic. Take this question we overheard in a university library: "Does anyone read encyclopediae these days?"

The rule of thumb: Generally, the Latin or Greek endings are used when speaking scientifically, otherwise the English *s* endings are used—but there are exceptions. If you don't want to sound either like one of the ignorami (or ignoramuses) or too stuffy, take heed of the following list showing some better-known Latin-origin (or Greek) singular words and their plurals and when to use them.

agendum / agenda: People say "agenda" for the singular as well as the plural now.

alumna / alumnae; alumnus / alumni: The *a* and *ae* refer to women; today most just use the masculine *us* and *i* versions.

appendix / appendices: Many people use the English "appendixes" as well as the Latin "appendices," so it's your call.

axis / axes: Here the Latin is better than the English "axises," which sounds weird.

cactus / cacti: "Cacti" is more commonly used, but "cactuses" is fine, too.

crisis / crises: The Latin plural is much better and clearer than the English plural "crisises."

datum / data: Almost everyone says "data" for both singular and plural. Saying "I found that datum interesting" makes you sound like a snob.

encyclopedia / encyclopediae: Again, unless you're an insufferable snob, say "encyclopedias."

formula / formulae: Scientists still use the Latin; many of us laypeople just say "formulas."

fungus / fungi: As with cacti / cactuses, you can also say "funguses," but "fungi" sounds fine, too.

hippopotamus / hippopotami: The Latin is technically correct, but just say "hippos."

index / indices: Both "indices" and "indexes" are commonly used.

memorandum / memoranda: The Latin plural is pretty widely used, but you can just say "memorandums" as well.

nucleus / nuclei: Use the Latin ending—almost no one says "nucleuses."

octopus / octopi / octopodes: The correct English plural is "octopuses," but almost everyone says (the incorrect) "octopi," a faux Latin word since *octopus* actually comes from the ancient Greek. So if you want to be super-correct, it's actually "octopodes." All of this reminds us of a truly dreadful joke. A Roman walks into a bar and asks for a martinus. "You mean a martini?" the bartender asks. The Roman replies, "If I wanted a double, I would have asked for it!"

hurdle / hurtle

"Unlike on Earth, solar storms involve 'drops' of plasma the size of Ireland hurdling down from the Sun's corona at a breakneck speed of 200,000 kilometers per hour."

—IFLSCIENCE! WEBSITE

Proper cosmically well-behaved solar-storm plasma drops *hurtle*, they don't *hurdle*. *Hurdling* means "jumping over hurdles," either literally (those upright frames found in track and field events) or figuratively (obstacles).

Nowadays, though, it seems many things besides plasma from the sun wrongly hurdle instead of hurtle. Taking a quick look through numerous novels, we found many characters "hurdling down" various streets, tunnels, paths, hallways, as well as down from trees, branches, ledges, and walls, and not hurdling where they should—on athletic fields. This mistake is such a common feature that it's unfair to single any specific modern novel out. However, we found this error in older books as well, including 1878 children's book *Spenser for Children* (a kiddified version of fourteenth-century poet Edmund Spenser's work—and a bit ambitious for a children's book). In it, a character "hurdled down stones." A contemporary reviewer complained, "Spenser uses quite enough queer forms without any fresh ones being fathered on him." We agree with the gist of this: why add to a reader's difficulties by misusing perfectly good words? So let's all differentiate *hurtle* and *hurdle*.

One quick note: *Hurtle* used to involve collisions, but now it doesn't necessarily, unless one hurtles *against* something. As for the related word *hurl*, one hurls (throws with force) a ball, one hurtles (speeds down) a street to catch a hurled ball, maybe after hurdling—i.e., jumping a few hurdles? No . . . that's pushing it.

hurdle (v): to jump over an obstacle
hurtle (v): to go very fast

---

hypothesis

"Hayao Miyazaki understands stories about children better than any filmmaker, period. That's my hypothesis—there is no other filmmaker living or dead that has a better grasp on how to realistically convey children on the big screen."

—CINAPSE FILM

According to physicist and science blogger Rhett Allain, *hypothesis* is "the worst science word ever! Well, not ever, but currently." He and many scientists concur: we laypeople use it incorrectly and it drives them crazy. While we sympathize with them, we personally think it's A-OK to use *hypothesis* unscientifically. But let's give them a few seconds here to get it off their scientific chests.

Nonscientists use *hypothesis* to mean "an educated guess," plain and simple. But to scientists, it's not that simple. Their *hypothesis* is based on careful observation and known facts, which will be subjected to testing to prove or disprove it. This testability angle is crucial in the scientific sense of the word, and it's the aspect that is missing from many people's use of *hypothesis*. People also use *hypothesis* as a replacement for *theory*, another problem for scientists, because a hypothesis can be refuted, while a theory stands up to current tests. A hypothesis *becomes* a theory; it isn't one to begin with.

Hypothesis, which began being used in English in the late sixteenth century, comes from the Middle French *hypothese,* via the Greek *hypothesis* (groundwork, foundation), a combination of *hypo-* (under) and *thesis* (a proposition). This fits with its technical meaning, since a *hypothesis* is literally the basis of a premise.

So while we think it is fine to use *hypothesis* as a stand-in for an educated guess, we suggest you think twice before using it this way in front of a scientist. We hypothesize that would make your life easier. No, wait, we *guess* it will.

hypothesis (n): premise based on careful observation and known facts; colloquially, an educated guess

hysterical / hilarious

"Ken Ludwig's Hysterical Comedy Opens in Santa Paula"

HEADLINE, *SANTA PAULA* [CA] *TIMES*

Does *hysterical* mean "funny"? Is it a substitute for *hilarious*?

According to the headline above about a "sidesplitting comedy," yes and yes. And according to the writers of tens of thousands of blogs, comments, letters, books, and articles on "hysterical" films, friends, and situations, ditto.

But according to most dictionaries, nope. It should be *hilarious. Hysterical* means "having uncontrolled extreme emotion, including uncontrollable laughter." It's usually not meant in the positive sense, as in watching a funny comedy, but in a quite negative sense of being out of control and upset, as this list of synonyms shows: overwrought, berserk, frenzied, frantic, wild, feverish, crazed.

Hysteria has a not-so-funny and misogynist past. It comes from the ancient Greek word *husterikós*, meaning "suffering in the womb," and indeed over the centuries an entire medical industry was built around diagnosing women (and only women) as "hysterical." Too much sexual desire? Hysterical. Too little sexual desire for an unattractive husband? Not his fault—hysterical wife. In fact, prominent British physician Havelock Ellis wrote in his famous *The Sexual Impulse in Women* that almost 75 percent of women suffered from hysteria. Fortunately, times have changed with the diagnosis and the medical use of the word. By the 1930s, the meaning of *hysteria* in the positive sense of happy, uncontrollable laughter took hold. Its use in this capacity has increased to such a degree that it's now almost everywhere— which is enough to make English speakers like us hysterical.

hysterical (adj): having uncontrolled extreme emotion
hilarious (adj): extremely funny

---

impact

"You have to see the connection between what we do and what it impacts on us and how it impacts around the world. So I ask you to support that."

—PUBLIC PAPERS OF THE PRESIDENTS OF THE UNITED STATES: WILLIAM J. CLINTON

No, Bill, we can't support that. "Impacts on" is clunky. Why not use "how it affects us" instead? Notwithstanding our objections, and those of many editors (albeit a steadily decreasing number), *impact* as a verb meaning "to affect" is here to stay. But let's complain about it anyway. . . .

The argument over *impact* as both noun and verb has been going on for decades. It came from the past participle of the Latin word *impingere* (to fasten, bring into violent contact, thrust on a person), thus its main meaning then and now—as a verb, "to come forcibly in contact with," as a noun, "a collision." All fine and dandy. But over the years, *impact* collided with a changing world, and some more meanings were added.

First, for the noun: *Impact* now can mean having a dramatic effect on someone.

In the 1960s, according to an *American Heritage* survey, this usage was frowned upon, but by 2015 a whopping 97 percent of the survey said, "Fine, why not?" So you can say that both an asteroid hitting Earth and an insult had an impact on you and not be considered a grammatical incompetent.

Impact used as a verb with the preposition "on," for example, "the insult impacting *on* me" is another matter. In the 2015 *American Heritage* survey, 78 percent disapproved, and so do we. But *impact* used transitively (without a preposition) meaning "to affect" was disapproved of by only 39 percent, down from 66 percent in 2001. So, sadly, resistance is probably futile.

impact (n) a collision; (v): to come forcibly in contact with; also having a dramatic effect upon

impending / pending

"However, the prospect of my impending marriage (to a lovely, understanding, open-minded and progressive straight cis-man) has forced me to clarify my perspectives. . . ."

—OFFBEAT BRIDE WEBSITE

Merriam-Webster's first definition of *impending* is "to hover threateningly." Since most brides presumably don't view marriage as an imminent horror, we'd use another word. How about her "pending" marriage to the lovely and progressive Mr. Wonderful? Unless . . . maybe he's not so wonderful after all? This sounds like the beginning of a Gothic novel.

Impending and *pending* are obviously closely related. Many dictionaries include *impending* to mean simply "something awaiting a conclusion," good or bad (or in other words, pending). However, we think it best to differentiate *impending* from its lesser twin because it has so many not-so-nice usages, as in "impending storms" or "impending stock market crashes."

Pending comes from the Latin *pendere* (to hang). It came into English with an alternate meaning of "not decided," as in a hung jury or "The case is pending." As for *impending*, with the tacked-on Latin prefix *im-* (actually *in-*, which changed to *im-*), it took the sense of overhanging, sometimes literally, as in this from an 1845 Senate report about clearing obstacles from rivers: ". . . the 'Heliopolis' removed from . . . the Mississippi 7 snags and 36 impending trees." But *impending* is now often used figuratively concerning imminent bad things about to happen (not that overhanging trees are good, either), as in this description from a Gothic novel: "Courted by fun-loving Philip, son of a powerful family, Ellen senses impending doom as a recurrent nightmare haunts her. . . ." And so we say: keep *impending* away from marriages and such unless you're writing your next bodice ripper.

impending (adj): of imminent danger
pending (adj): imminent, not decided

imply / infer

"The action then shifts without a moment's pause to a bank robbery in Queens, with a sly racial commentary inferred by having Connie and Nick hold up an African-American cashier while wearing masks, sunglasses, and hoodies that give them the appearance of black men."

—*HOLLYWOOD REPORTER*

We are not going to imply anything. And you don't have to infer anything. *Imply* and *infer* are two different words, quasi opposites in a way.

They both concern communicating and understanding information. But when you imply, you're the speaker. You're *giving* the information. When you infer, you're the listener or the reader *receiving* the information. *Imply* means "to suggest something or hint at it without saying it outright." *Infer* means "to conclude something based on signals or evidence you've picked up, ones that aren't explicitly expressed."

In spite of their distinct meanings, a lot of people use *infer* when they mean *imply*, making it common enough for some dictionaries to include "hint" or "imply" as a later definition for *infer*. Thankfully, some of them, like the *American Heritage Dictionary*, list it as a usage problem.

A look at their origins underscores their differences. *Imply* comes from the French *emplie-r* (to enfold, enwrap) by way of the Latin *implicare* (to fold into, involve). When it first appeared in about 1400, it meant "to involve something unstated as a logical consequence." After 1580, the now-common meaning of "to hint at" emerged. As for *infer*, it evolved from the Latin *inferre* (to deduce, conclude) and meant what it means today from the 1520s on.

And there you have it. On the positive side of things, when we plugged *infer* and *inferred* into Google news, more often than not it was used correctly. What are the implications of this? We'll leave it up to you to infer.

imply (v): to insinuate
infer (v): to draw conclusions based on evidence

---

in regard to

"Trump: US in 'good position' in regards to North Korea"
—HEADLINE, ABC NEWS

In regard to the statement above, it is incorrect. It shouldn't be "in regards to," it should be "in regard to." (But even though that singular "regard" is correct, why not keep the sentence shorter and snappier and say "regarding" or "concerning" or "about"?)

"In regards to" with the *s* is exceedingly common. We found it (mis)used in song titles, book titles, newspaper and magazine articles, and in basic usage, including questions on reddit and Quora. We also found "*with* regards to" instead of "with regard to" all over the place as well—in an article from the *International Journal of Higher Education*, sports websites like Sportsnet, even, sadly enough, on a good grammar website (that shall remain nameless) in a discussion of another grammatical matter.

For the record, *regards* with the *s* is correct in the phrase "as regards," where *regard* is a verb. As regards to (we couldn't resist) the phrases "in regard to" and "with regard to," *regard* is a noun, and the singular—without the *s*—should always be used. The only exception is when sending someone good wishes—"best regards"—or giving your regards to, say, Broadway, as in the song. After all, you probably wouldn't want to wish Broadway only one regard.

in regard to: regarding (no such phrase as "in regards to")

---

incredulous / incredible

"A few short weeks ago, coming from a background, believe me, as conservative and traditionally grounded in scientific fact as any of you, I began an experiment in, incredulous as it may sound, the reanimation of dead tissue."

—DR. FREDERICK FRANKENSTEIN [GENE WILDER] IN *YOUNG FRANKENSTEIN*

Incredible as it may sound, Herr Dr. Frankenstein should not have said "incredulous."

Incredulous means "skeptical, unwilling to admit or accept what is offered as true"—and refers to a person's skeptical response to something. Dr. Frankenstein used the wrong word to refer to his remarkable reanimation of dead tissue. It was *incredible*.

It's all a matter of perspective, at least in current preferred usage. Frankenstein or his audience can be incredulous since they're people, but things or ideas can't be incredulous. In earlier English, *incredible* and *incredulous* were far more interchangeable, as in this 1533 diplomatic letter: "The Pope, whos Sight is incredulous quick, eyed me, and that divers tymes." We'd now say "incredibly" (and while we were at it, we'd make a number of spelling changes). A few years later, good old Will Shakespeare in *Twelfth Night* also plopped *incredulous* in where today we'd say *incredible*: "No obstacle, no incredulous or unsafe circumstance."

But times are changing once more. Some dictionaries include *incredulous* as a substitute for *incredible*, although others are holdouts. But *incredible* is the usual usage for things that are, well, incredible. Like the reanimation of dead tissue.

incredulous (adj): unbelieving
incredible (adj): beyond belief, amazing

---

ingenious / ingenuous

"Now, though, a pair of Canadian engineers have come up with an ingenious way of using the heat of the sun to drive the process."

—THE ECONOMIST

"*The Economist* proclaimed one of his first desalination inventions as 'an ingenuous way of using the heat of the sun.'"

—CANADIAN MANUFACTURERS AND EXPORTERS EMERGING LEADERS WEBSITE

The *Economist* said "ingenious," but the Canadian Manufacturers and Exporters website says "ingenuous." Who's right?

The *Economist*, unless the Canadian Manufacturers think their inventors and engineers are "naive, candid, innocent, and childlike," the definition of *ingenuous*. Cute childlike engineers . . . ? We think (like the *Economist*) that engineers and inventors are *ingenious*—"clever, original, and inventive."

The ingenious/ingenuous confusion is common and problematic. The words are almost opposite in meaning yet are often used as synonyms, as in the example given. The two words stem from the Latin root verb *gignere* (to give birth), but both come from two different Latin nouns based on this verb. *Ingenuous* evolved from the Latin noun *ingenuus* (born in a place, natural, freeborn). Since freeborn people were thought to be noble minded and not afraid to speak the truth, *ingenuous* came to mean "candid, frank, forthright." After it came into English via the French, it gradually came to mean not only "candid," but "artless, a little naive, innocent," the primary meaning it has today. *Ingenious* also came via the same root verb through another derived noun meaning "inborn"—by the time it moved over into early English it meant, as it does now, "skillful, crafty, clever."

But throughout history, the two words often have been used interchangeably—here's a "mistake" by none other than William Shakespeare in *Love's Labor Lost*: "Yf their Sonnes be ingenous, they shal want no instruction" (Actually, he misused *ingenuous* three times, according to the *OED*, but who's counting?)

ingenious (adj): clever, skillful
ingenuous (adj): naive, innocent

inherent / inherit

"Capitalism will never stop or 'reform' the depravity inherit in the system."

—*FOCUS ON SOCIALISM: THE POLITICAL JOURNAL OF CANADIANS FOR PEACE AND SOCIALISM*

This is an odd one. We never expected to find people incorrectly using *inherit* for *inherent*, but once we saw it, we seemed to see it everywhere.

Inherent describes something that is a permanent or essential attribute or element, as in "Children have an inherent sense of right and wrong." *Inherit* means "to receive as an heir or get from parents or ancestors," as in "Children inherit their inherent sense of right or wrong from their parents."

Clearly different meanings—but with similar spellings and sounds, it's easy to see how they came to be confused. We found fewer errors of confusing *inherit* for *inherent*, but a surprising number came from various universities (several from computing departments). Then there was an example from a publication with this long title: "Interesting Facts About the 1611 King James Version of the Bible (dedicated to those who erroneously and carnally idolize that particular translation)." The offending passage reads, "When the King James Translation finally began to be published and widely used in the United States, one could correct some of these faulty translations that are inherit within it. . . ."

No, it should be *"inherent* within it." This is a case where correct usage is particularly important: when criticizing another's translation into English, it's best to strive for correctness in one's own. (Which we must add is a lesson we're constantly relearning ourselves. This is why we value copy editors—*after* they've finished correcting us!)

inherent (adj): of an attribute that exists within
inherit (v): to receive as heir, to get from one's parents or ancestors

---

inter / intern

"[Kim Il-Sung's] body is interned in the Kumsusan Palace of the Sun, where it lies preserved for people to see."

—*DAILY EXPRESS* [UK]

Poor Kim Il-Sung. According to the sentence above, after the dictator of North Korea died, instead of being buried he was either confined as a political prisoner or forced to work as a medical trainee. Pretty tough for a deceased autocrat. The *Express* copy editor missed the incorrect extra *n* in this account of Kim. To *inter*, which means "to bury," has no *n* at the end. To *intern*—which principally means "to work as a trainee to gain experience (often medical)" or "to be confined"—has that vital *n*. (There's also a noun form, an *intern*, who is . . . guess what? Someone who interns.)

The error above is obviously rather minor. It's easy by context to see whether the writer is referring to the dear departed or some medical practitioner. But it's an important distinction if the person you're referring to is dead. We've heard this word misused at funerals, where it detracts from the solemnity of the occasion and conjures up visions of the living dead.

Inter comes from the Latin *in* (into) and *terra* (land)—"into the land"—so it's easy to see how it means "to bury." *Intern* came from the Latin word *internus*, meaning "internal"; it got its current meaning from the idea of working inside a house or office. Particularly nowadays, with all the work piled onto medical interns, you could say they're often figuratively buried (interred).

inter: (v): to bury
intern (v): to work as a trainee, to confine someone; (n): trainee, often medical

---

ironic

"It's ironic that we rush through being 'single' as if it's some disease or malady to get rid of or overcome."

—*WILDFLOWER*

If you've been using *ironic* correctly all the time, we applaud you. *Ironic* is one of the sneakiest, slipperiest, most easily misused words. This is because it has such a vague, sneaky, slippery, and easily misconstrued definition.

Basically, it means "saying something (or noticing something) that is the opposite of what is expected, with a funny or sarcastic twist." And the key is that concept of *opposite*. Yet people chuck it into conversations to mean a myriad of non-opposite things—from odd to interesting to funny, even to strangely sad, as in the above. But *irony* is something very specific. It's not a catchall word you use to mean "gee, I didn't expect that" or "isn't that odd that that happened?"

Irony has been misused for many years, probably ever since it emerged back in ancient Greece, evolving from the *eiron*, a comic character in plays who would understate his abilities and so manage to vanquish his arrogant opponent.

Identifying irony can be confusing. It has elements of the paradoxical, sarcastic, unexpected, and humorous but with—dare we say—an ironic twist. Perhaps the best explanation comes from George Carlin in his book *Brain Droppings*:

> *If a diabetic, on his way to buy insulin, is killed by a runaway truck, he is the victim of an accident. If the truck was delivering sugar, he is the victim of an oddly poetic coincidence. But if the truck was delivering insulin, ah! Then he is the victim of an irony.*

ironic (adj): referring to something that is cruelly or funnily opposite of what is expected

jealous / envious

"A close friend sent me this text after a party at our home: 'You look amazing, your baby is beautiful, your friends are hilarious, your husband is a dream, and I am so jealous of your house."

—FORBES.COM

Nowadays you can almost always substitute *jealous* or *jealousy* for *envious* or *envy* and no annoying grammar extremist will correct you. But there are subtle differences. *Envy* is best used when someone doesn't have—and wants—something someone else has: "I am so envious of your house." Many linguists say you can substitute *jealous*, although others, including us, don't think it sounds quite right.

Jealousy is best used with romantic or relationship-oriented feelings, as in "He was a jealous boyfriend." Using *envious* instead doesn't work quite as well: the possessively personal and suspicious relationship aspect is subtly reduced. You may even be left thinking the boyfriend was envious about personal possessions rather than his girlfriend. That said, both words are really quite interchangeable—except if you speak with a psychiatrist.

Professional psychologists and sociologists are adamant. The authoritative *Handbook of the Sociology of Emotions* sternly states that "most important here is that envy is *not* the same as jealousy." They note that one difference between envy and jealousy is numerical. Jealousy usually involves a ménage à trois: three people (or three "poles" of people—me, my significant other, and the person(s) he/she is now interested in). Envy usually only involves two (me and that rich person who has all the money I'd like to have.) For more on this, you can read *The Psychology of Jealousy and Envy,* which devotes nine whole chapters to jealousy, and only one to envy (and two chapters to both.) Enough to make Envy envious of Jealousy.

jealous (adj): usually romantic envy
envious (adj): wanting something someone else has

just deserts

"As for the 'cowards' and 'opportunists' who aided and abetted Trump, there will be a day of reckoning when they will get their just desserts, we are told."

—*WASHINGTON EXAMINER*

Ice cream or cake? It should be "just *deserts*" not "just desserts." It's only a silly little *s*, but persnickety types like us don't approve of that extra sibilant. The *desert* part means neither tasty desserts nor those dry sandy places. Instead, *desert* means "deserved," and so *just deserts* means "justly or rightly deserved." The *desert* comes from the Latin past participle of *deservire* (to deserve), via the French. We rarely encounter this kind of desert in everyday speech, but it survives in philosophy and law, as in this from the *Stanford Encyclopedia of Philosophy*: ". . . several philosophers have advocated versions of the idea that justice obtains when goods and evils are distributed according to desert." *Stanford* goes on (and on), but for our purposes that's enough.

A caveat: In a certain sense, "just desserts" can be correct. It is now wryly used (and overused) as a title to dessert-related cookbooks, websites, articles, and shows: "just desserts" as meaning "just desert desserts," or in other words richly deserved desserts. Google "just desserts" and you'll find a plethora of these titles celebrating tantalizing chocolate cake recipes and the like. The sad part to this is that you'll also find entries by more than a few unfortunate souls who have made the opposite mistake, offering up food recipes under the title "Just Deserts," which feature "delicious deserts." Sandy chocolate cakes? Not for us.

just deserts (not "just desserts," n): what one deserves

less / fewer

Even *Washington Post* copy editors aren't perfect. Technically, it should be "fewer people," not "less people." Why? It all depends on if and what you're counting. Here are the basic rules for when to use less or fewer:

1. Use "fewer" for numbered, countable things, especially people or other plural nouns ("Fewer than twenty people were in the library."

2. Use "less" for things that can't be counted (at least reasonably), as in "there's less sand at the beach." Often these uncountable things are singular collective nouns for plural things, like sand.

3. Use "less" with numbers when they are a single or total unit, usually with "than," as in "Less than 50 percent of us went to the game." This can be tricky, because often you'll see numbers in the plural, as in "He has less than a million dollars," that presumably have been counted (as in rule 1). But since here we're really talking about *total* amounts of nonhuman things, use "less." (Don't blame us—that's the rule. Still, it's all less—not fewer!—difficult than you'd think.)

That said, many people make mistakes: for example, the Oxford English Corpus found that "less people" was used 21 percent of the time. Although we recommend following these rules, they're not hard and fast, and they're mostly due to an obscure English grammarian, Robert Baker, who opined that *fewer* when referring to a number sounded more "elegant" than *less*. He didn't say it was a rule, but others took up the idea, and it's been causing agita among English speakers ever since.

less (adj, adv): a smaller quantity of (usually things that can't be counted, or a single unit)
fewer (adj): a smaller quantity of (usually things that can be counted)

---

limn

"But her skill at being so convincing as a psychopath also allows her to limn everything from *Girls* to *Masters of Sex* to *Good Behavior* to Chekhov's *The Seagull* on Broadway."

—*VARIETY*

We don't think we're going out on a, um, limn (groan) when we say that, like bad puns, people either love or hate the word *limn*. Writer James Parker called it a "disgusting verb"; critic Michael Dirda described it as an "ugly, pushy" word; writer David Foster Wallace said using it was "just off-the-charts pretentious"; and writer Ben Yagoda said it "had never been said aloud in the history of English." And when the *Baltimore Sun* used it in a headline ("Opposing votes limn difference in race"), readers revolted.

On the flip side, you have those literary types who can't stop limning all over the joint—like former *New York Times* book critic Michiko Kakutani, who apparently never met a limn she didn't like to the point where she was credited with reinvigorating the rather archaic word. We'll admit we fall into the not-crazy-about-limn camp. And it's even worse when people use it incorrectly, which is quite common.

Limn usually means "to portray or depict in words." It initially meant "to illuminate," as in illuminating a manuscript and, logically, it came from the Old French *luminer,* out of the Medieval Latin *luminare* (to make light). So limning something makes (figurative) light of something or, visually, outlines it in light. It does not mean "to cover, to skirt around," or any of the other problematic usages we've seen that make us dislike the word even more.

What a shame. We'd like to be glad that a once-moribund word has regained popularity. In other words, if life hands you limns, make . . . you know.

limn (v): to portray or depict, usually in words

literally / figuratively

"That's the type of coverage that CNN offers in this presidential race as they literally kiss Hillary Clinton's ass and Obama's ass every day."

—FOX NEWS HOST SEAN HANNITY, SPEAKING TO COLLEAGUES, AS REPORTED IN POLITICO.COM

Literally means "in a literal manner or sense," or in other words, *exactly,* to the letter. So does Sean Hannity think that CNN reporters are, *actually,* uh, kissing . . . ?

We hope not. We're taking a wild guess that he was using *literally* in its now infamous and opposite second definition, *figuratively.*

In the good old (probably mythical) days of English, when words weren't allowed to mean their opposite, there was a generally recognized difference: *literally* meant "actually," the opposite of *figuratively*; *figuratively* meant "metaphorically," the opposite of *literally*. If people said, "He's literally on fire," they meant a person was actually burning. If they said he was figuratively on fire, they meant he was angry.

Yes, many famous writers literally have used *literally* in its second (figurative) sense, like F. Scott Fitzgerald in *The Great Gatsby*: "He literally glowed. . . ." But writerly excesses or flourishes aside, both words were useful with their distinctive meanings.

But in the early 1960s, confusion between the two literally (figuratively speaking) exploded. Many dictionaries began defining *literally* as "in effect" or "very" and, by the 1970s, also as "figuratively," albeit as a second definition.

We think having a word also meaning its exact opposite is dumb. Without the distinction between *literally* and *figuratively*, we have to pause when someone runs in and says, "Sean is on fire!" Of course, there's always context to figure out the correct meaning, but context can be deceiving and meanwhile, our poor friend may be literally on fire.

literally (adv): actually
figuratively (adv): not actually, metaphorically

loath / loathe

Sharp-eyed copy editors usually catch the loath-loathe confusion the *Daily Planet* editors missed, but we are not loath to say that a lot of us don't. In the above example, it should be *loath* (disinclined) rather than *loathe* (to hate). It's very common confusion. Many angry computer users post that they are "loathe" to do something for fear of losing data. Since *loathe* means hatred, maybe the computer users are subliminally channeling their (very often justified) hatred of their computer or Microsoft Windows. But as with the above, *loath* without an *e* is the word they should be using.

The problem is that, while they're pronounced differently, they're not only similar in spelling, they're the same in origin. *Loathe* comes from the Old English *lað* (hated, hateful, hostile, repulsive), via Old Saxon, Frisian, Old Norse, and a bunch of other Nordic languages, and before that from an old Proto-Indo-European root *leit* (to detest)—and so does *loath*. They began to differ in medieval England in the 1300s or so, when *loath* without the *e* took on a meaning we have today, as in Chaucer's translation of *The Consolation of Philosophy* by Roman philosopher Boethius: "She lyueth looþ of hir lyf"— the "loo" with the funny looking *b* is actually *loath* (trust us). Shortly thereafter, this use of *loath*, meaning "averse," faded, and in the 1700s, few people would be loath to do anything.

But in the 1800s, antiquarian-minded scholars began using *loath* again, and soon, the rest of the English-speaking world as well. As for us, we are loath to say anything further.

loath (adj): averse, disinclined
loathe (v): to hate

---

luxuriant / luxurious

"You cannot fail to be seduced by the authenticity and charm of the peaceful and luxuriant Hotel La Colombière."

—AD FOR HOTEL LA COLOMBIÈRE, GENEVA

Unfortunately, if what the advertisement above is saying is true, we will most certainly fail to be seduced. The hotel seems better suited for a low-budget horror movie. *Luxuriant* means "characterized by profuse, vigorous, or abundant growth." It's most often used to characterize vegetation, as in, "The tropical island was completely covered by a luxuriant jungle." This is fine for a tropical island, but not inside one's hotel, with strange things inside growing . . . and growing. . . .

To avoid the possible mental picture of a hotel smothered in prolific jungle vines (which seem particularly incongruous and frightening in Switzerland), the advertisement should have used the word *luxurious*. Both words seem interchangeable and, not surprisingly, they come from the same old Latin word *luxus* (excess), via *luxuria* (luxury, extravagance). This makes sense in terms of their similarities in meaning: *luxuriant*, "a luxury of growth"—and *luxurious*, "a luxury of comfort, wealth, or opulence."

Today, some of the more descriptive dictionaries include *luxuriant* as meaning "luxurious," but usually not as a preferred definition. Most or at least many (we haven't counted) people still frown on this substitution, as do we. *Luxuriant* and *luxurious* are two different and evocative words, both useful. Why not use each for a specific meaning? We might even say that English is a luxuriant language, and can afford the luxury of specified definitions.

luxuriant (adj): having abundant or lush growth
luxurious (adj): of or pertaining to luxury

---

meretricious / meritorious

"You see I'm trapped between morbid curiosity and a hard place. A hard, barren place where the meretricious blogger heroically promotes the underdog, trying to bring lesser known gems to the masses, promoting the medium they love in the form that they love."

—HUFFINGTON POST

Meretricious is an unfair word—it sounds like it's good when it's not. It seems like it should mean "meritorious, deserving of honor or merit," as the HuffPo blogger seems to think. One would assume that *merit* is its root word, but it isn't, although both originally evolved from the same Latin verb *mereri* (to be hired). But *meretricious* doesn't mean anything like merit. It actually refers to something that appears attractive but has no value or integrity, or something gaudy or insincere.

The word *meretricious* is linked to prostitution. It comes directly from the Latin feminine noun *meretrix* (a Roman lady of the night), from *mereri*. (Interestingly, while the word *prostitute* also comes from Latin, it wasn't used by the Romans.) English had an archaic meaning of *meretricious*—"relating to prostitutes," as used by Sir Francis Bacon in *New Atlantis*: "The Delight in Meretricious Embracements, (wher sinne is turned into Art)."

To make things a little more difficult, there's another meaning of *meretricious* that is derived from this sexual aspect—you'll see it in legal documents. "A meretricious relationship" is not a tasteless relationship but a stable, marital-like relationship where both parties cohabit but aren't legally married. So nowadays you can have a meritorious meretricious relationship that isn't meretricious. Try saying that to a judge.

meretricious (adj): something that has no value in spite of its appealing appearance

meritorious (adj): deserving of reward or praise

---

meteor / meteorite

"Did UFO 'hit' Russian meteorite blasting it to smithereens? Conspiracy theorists' extraordinary claim after new footage emerges."

—*DAILY MAIL* [UK]

We can confidently say that absolutely no UFO hit a meteorite in the sky over Russia on linguistic *grounds*. The key is that last word. *Meteorites* are "post-impact objects from space," i.e., they're on the ground. Meteors are in the sky. They're the flash of light that we see, also called a shooting star. The authoritative

NASA Hubble blog says that meteors are *only* that flash of light, not the glowing solid object causing that flash, but many dictionaries disagree and say that you can call both the flash of light and the glowing sky object falling to the earth "meteors."

Why is *meteorite* so commonly and incorrectly used for *meteor*? One astronomy blog blamed it on "people who want to appear more intelligent than they really are" who love extra syllables, and now it's been picked up by the rest of us who never learned the difference.

But astronomers to the rescue. They have helpfully explained the distinction with other space objects in detail:

asteroids—larger space rocks, which mostly come from the asteroid belt between Jupiter and Mars.

comets—asteroid-like objects covered with ice, methane, ammonia.

meteoroids—rocks (smaller than a kilometer) whizzing around in space; before they hit the earth's atmosphere and become meteors and then hit the earth and become meteorites.

And for those exceptionally technical types, how about a boloid or a bolide? That's an extremely bright meteor or sky fireball, caused when a meteoroid explodes in the earth's atmosphere.

meteor (n): a shooting star; a small piece of space rock or metal that
   enters the earth's atmosphere
meteorite (n): a meteor that has hit the ground

methodology

"We have not only failed to require that the IRS utilize only
secure and reliable authentication methodologies but we
have also given it carte blanche to determine what burden a
taxpayer must bear to overcome this evidentiary hurdle."

—SENATOR JOHN ASHCROFT (R-MISSOURI) IN THE
CONGRESSIONAL RECORD, IRS HEARINGS

Methodology is an annoying word that should be kept in its place.
But it has oozed into a lot of places, especially into government
documents and Big Business annual reports, probably because it
sounds official, important . . . and pretentious. For fun (we have
odd definitions of fun), we did a Google search for *methodology*
coupled with another puffy pretentious word, *utilize*, to see
if we could find them both used in the *same* sentence. The
senatorial example above is the first we found—a home run in
the Very Bad English World Series.

The senator should have used the word *method*, which
we're sure he knows means "a procedure" or "a way of doing
something." *Methodology* technically isn't just another way
of saying this. Instead, *methodology* best means, in *Merriam-
Webster's* succinct definition, "the analysis of the principles or
procedures of inquiry in a particular field." The *-logy* tacked
onto the end of *method* transforms the word into *the study* of
methods or ways of doing something. (The *-logy* ending comes
from the ancient Greek *logia*, "explanation," "the study of"), so
Egyptology is the study of (ancient) Egypt, and methodology is
the study of certain methods.

Methodology has its place in English—it's just that it should
stay there and not substitute for *method*. One interesting

note: The IRS itself, in contrast to the senator speaking about the IRS, almost always uses the word *method* instead of *methodology*. Count on tax professionals to use a more economical word.

methodology (n): technically, the study of methods or systems

---

mitigate / militate

"Marine Reserves Help Mitigate Against Climate Change, Say Scientists

An international team of scientists has concluded that 'highly protected' marine reserves can help mitigate the effects of climate change and suggests that these areas be expanded and better managed throughout the world."

—PHYS.ORG WEBSITE

The headline writer was wrong—but, interestingly, the article underneath used *mitigate* correctly.

Here's a tip: When you see or hear "mitigate against," it's most likely wrong. It probably should be "militate against." *Mitigate* means "to make soft or mild, to lessen or reduce the effect." *Militate* means "to be a powerful factor in preventing something from happening," and is most often used with "against." *Mitigate* isn't. So the headline above, which uses *mitigate*, says (incorrectly) that "Marine reserves help lessen against climate change." Doesn't make much sense in our book. *Militate* against (fighting climate change) or *mitigate* (reducing climate change) should have been used instead.

Militate comes from the Latin, and as you might guess, originally meant "to serve as a soldier." It's easy to see how the meaning migrated to include fighting against (or more rarely for) a cause. *Mitigate* is also from the Latin; the *miti* part came from *mitis* (sweet, juicy, ripe, soft, and yielding). Soft, yielding fruit and tough soldiering are not all that interchangeable, and neither are the words.

We concede that "mitigate against" in recent years has become more accepted, but it's still clunky and technically incorrect. Yes, William Faulkner used it once (in an article in the *American Mercury*) and so did the *Times of London* back in 1963. But "mitigate against" seems to be mostly the province of bureaucrats and tax lawyers, who are not generally known for their limpid prose.

mitigate (v): to lessen the effect of, to soften
militate (v): to exert power or influence to prevent something

---

momentarily

"It was as if I'm calling Direct TV or Time Warner Cable and getting a message, 'Please hold on the line, the next available operator will be with you momentarily.'"

—NBC NEW YORK WEBSITE

This is a word less often misused in print, more often misused in regular conversation, and most often misused by communications behemoths. How often have we heard that canned voice—"Someone will be with you momentarily"— while on hold with the cable or phone company?

Of course, that's technically wrong. We refer not to the length of time someone actually takes to get to you (although it's never "just a moment"), but to the use of *momentarily*.

Traditionally, technically, it means "*for* a moment," not *in* a moment. Something happens momentarily; it lasts for a second.

As with other words, the more time goes on, the more accepted the newer nontraditional meaning becomes. This is neatly demonstrated by the *American Heritage* Usage Panel, which shows momentarily-as-in-*in-a-moment* having a 59 percent acceptance rate in 1988 and an 83 percent acceptance rate in 2013. And the venerable *OED* includes "at any moment; in a moment, soon" as its fourth definition of *momentarily*, but notes that it is chiefly North American. It also notes that this usage isn't as modern as one might think. It first appeared in print in Augusta Jane Evans's 1869 novel, *Vashti*: "Robert is bringing her home as carefully as possible, and you may expect them momentarily."

Some language experts advise using *presently* instead. But that seems awkward to us. So is it okay to use *momentarily* to mean "in a moment"? We'll get back to you momentarily—[pause]—which is to say, why not?

momentarily (adv): for a moment

---

moot

"The kick hit a Cowboy players' [sic] leg before it traveled the required ten yards. So the fact that the Cowboys recovered it was moot."

—SPORTING NEWS

The use of *moot* is, well, moot. And, no, we're not being cute. What we're saying is that the meaning of moot is open to debate—which is, actually, the time-honored definition of moot.

This can provoke very heated arguments, which is fitting since *moot* began as a legal term.

More specifically, it started out in twelfth-century England as a noun, meaning "a meeting, usually a legislative or judicial one." It entered into the legal lexicon as an adjective in the 1500s, meaning "a case proposed for discussion at a moot," which segued into the current meaning—"something that is debatable, open to argument." But by the mid-1800s, it also began being used to mean "something *not* worth considering." The idea was that something debatable and inconclusive is of no practical value and isn't worth bothering with. So sometimes *moot* even is used to mean "definitely *not* debatable" because the point is so immaterial. This change in meaning is primarily North American, and it is one that has stuck, although language purists argue about it. (Fitting for a word based in the legal profession!)

What to do? This is one of those cases where avoidance might serve you best. Otherwise, sharpen your debating skills and be prepared to defend your *moot*. In other words, the point is, yes, moot. (Side note: At least it's not "mute," the newest twist on the moot front. Yes, some people have taken to referring to "mute points." We're going to remain silent about them.)

moot (adj): debatable

myself

We have real concerns, too . . . about how often we keep seeing and hearing *myself* when a *me* or an *I* should be used. They throw in *myself* because *me* and *I* are so confusing. Which to choose? I? Me? Help! So *myself* is the easy way out. The problem is, it's often the ungrammatical way out.

Here's a quick grammar lesson: *Myself* (like the other -self/-selves pronouns: herself, himself, etc.) is a reflexive pronoun. This means it is the object of a sentence, never the subject. The easiest way to see if it's right without really thinking is to take out the other person in your sentence. "My partner and myself went out to dinner" sounds okay, but then take out your partner. You wouldn't say, "Myself went out to dinner." (At least we hope you wouldn't.)

That said, using *myself* instead of *I* or *me* is certainly common, and has been for many years. None other than statesman Benjamin Disraeli, who was known for his eloquence, used this form, as in this 1878 speech when he returned from the Congress of Berlin: "Lord Salisbury and myself have brought you back peace—but a peace I hope with honour."

So you're not in bad company should you use it. But the general rule of thumb, with which we agree, is that, because it's an informal usage and technically incorrect, it's better suited to conversation than writing. And with that, ourselves are going to move on.

myself (*pron*): reflexive pronoun of "me," also used to strengthen "I," as in "I myself"

TO ME OR NOT TO ME:
THE I/ME, HE/HIM, SHE/HER, WE/US ISSUE

"Billy, this is your decision, and whatever the decision is,
you know it's fine with your mother and I."

—BILLY BEANE'S FATHER IN THE FILM *MONEYBALL*

But it is not fine with we. That's because it should be "your mother
and me." Yes, Billy Beane's dad has fallen into the trap many people
fall into: thinking that "I" sounds more erudite than "me." And, of
course, they end up sounding less erudite.

Blame teachers and other grammar sticklers for doing their job
too well. They have been so strident about the incorrect usage of
"me" (as in "Don't say 'you and me are going,' say 'you and I are
going'") that people now chuck out all of the me's and the I's then
have it. Problem is, there is a right time to use "me" and a wrong
time to use "I."

This shoving of "I" in when "me" is actually right is called a
"hypercorrection," which, as you would guess, occurs when people
overcorrect a perceived error. They think they are adhering to a
grammatical rule by doing so, but instead are committing a grammatical
mistake. (The I/me confusion is the most common hypercorrection.
Tossing in "whom" willy-nilly instead of "who" is another.)

In standard usage, I, we, he, she, and they are subjective pronouns,
used when the pronoun is the subject of a verb. (Jane and I/we/
he/she/they walked to the door.) Me, us, him, her, and them are
objective pronouns, used when the pronoun is the object of a verb—
when the verb is doing something to someone or something. (The
dog followed Jane and me/us/him/her/them to the door). Me/us, etc.
are also used after prepositions, where they're also the object. (Joe
walked to the door with Jane and me/us/him/her/them).

But people get confused, especially when there is more than one person or subject in the sentence. Probably the simplest way to determine which pronoun to use is to cut the other ones and see if "I" (or we, he, etc.) works. Using our *Moneyball* example, "It's fine with your mother and I" then becomes "It's fine with I." Wrong! It should be "me," although some people now argue that since so many people misuse "I," it's okay. Us thinks them's wrong.

While it has become more and more common to hear "I" when "me" is preferred, it's not a new issue at all. Back in 1568, playwright Ben Jonson, in his *Every Man in His Humour*, wrote "Musco has been with my cousin and I all this day." William Shakespeare was rather sloppy with his pronouns as well. Take this line from *The Merchant of Venice:* "Sweet Bassanio, . . . all debts are cleared between you and I." (Perhaps Will should have taken a few more moments to ponder the concept of "to me or not to me. . . .")

nauseous / nauseated

"It makes me mildly nauseous to think we might have had some impact on the election."

—FBI DIRECTOR JAMES COMEY TO SENATE JUDICIARY COMMITTEE, AS QUOTED ON CNBC.COM

We can convict the former FBI director on a technicality. He should have said, "It makes me feel mildly nauseated," if he wanted to follow the laws of correct grammatical usage. What's the difference? *Nauseous* refers to something *causing* someone to have nausea; *nauseated* means *having* that feeling.

From the beginning, both words have dealt with feeling sick. They are both based on the noun *nausea*, which came from the Latin *nausea* (seasickness), from the ancient Greek *nausi* or *nautia* (seasickness, or simply disgust or loathing), which ultimately came from *naus* (ship).

Nauseous came about first, appearing in 1613, and soon acquired the meaning "causing nausea," which is still its main definition today. But in the nineteenth century, it was also used in the United States to mean "affected with nausea or distaste"— yes, much like the "wrong" meaning today. And then there's *nauseated,* which entered the language in the seventeenth century, and, interestingly, initially meant . . . "causing nausea." But by the mid-1700s, it had become "suffering from nausea," which is where it pretty much stayed.

So how much of a grammatical crime did the then FBI director commit by misusing *nauseous*? Garner's *Modern American Usage* says it's no big deal—only "die hard snoots" notice the difference, but the *Chicago Manual of Style* prefers to keep the distinction. Our verdict: a misdemeanor only. After all, it's the feeling that counts.

nauseous (adj): refers to something causing nausea
nauseated (adj): feeling sick to one's stomach

---

noisome / noisy

"It is so good to hear the noisome sounds of young lives excitedly gathering to discover God's great love for them at Siloam."

—SILOAM BAPTIST CHURCH WEBSITE

We truly hope the Siloam Baptist pastor who wrote these words didn't think that the "sounds of young lives" he was hearing at his church were annoying, noxious, or harmful, and that the kids were foul smelling. But that's what *noisome* essentially means: "smelly or annoying."

Those kids may not be noisome, but the word itself is. The *nois* seems to be a truncated form of *noise*, like the *nois-* in *noisy*. But it isn't. *Noisome* didn't evolve from "noise" at all. It came from the Old French word *anoier* (to annoy). When it came into English, it got modified to "noye." Then, with the added suffix *-some* (as in tiresome, awesome, etc., meaning "characterized by"), it became *noysome* and then *noisome*—"something annoying, characterized by foulness, noxiousness, or annoyance, particularly relating to bad smells or things injurious to health and well-being."

Since most people are not etymologists or students of language, it's easy to assume *noisome* is just a classier way of saying "noisy" and to use it that way. In fact, type in "noisome din" or "noisome sounds" in Google, and you'll come up with a plethora of examples.

Several hundred years ago, you probably could have gotten away with that if you were in Scotland, according to an 1825 Scottish lexicon, which defines *noisome* as "noisy." But unless you're an antiquarian Scot reliving auld highland life, *noisome* has no relation to *noisy*. If for some reason you want to use a word similar to *noisome* that means "noisy," the *OED* suggests the word *noisesome*. But that's a really noisome word.

noisome (adj): smelly, annoying
noisy (adj): full of noise

---

nonplussed

"Over the past three years, [New York Giants quarterback Eli] Manning has given New York the impression that a dirty bomb could detonate in his locker and he would stand there nonplussed."

—*NEW YORK POST*

This quote actually means that if a dirty bomb exploded in quarterback Eli Manning's locker he would be very upset, maybe even scream a little. Which is probably true, but not the point that the *Post* was trying to make about the calm, cool, and collected QB.

No, *nonplussed* does not mean "calm," cool, and collected," even though many people seem to think so. Instead it means "very surprised and perturbed." The confusion over *nonplussed* for most of us comes from that *non-*. It's a prefix that, when tacked on to "plussed," seems to mean that you're "not plussed." "Plussed" must mean upset or something like that. Right? Wrong! Plussed doesn't mean anything in English. But *nonplussed* does.

Most experts think that *nonplussed* comes from the Latin *non plus* (no more, no further) and from there it evolved into an archaic English verb *nonplus* (unable to go further). It was used in early modern English to mean having one's thoughts brought to a halt. In other words, someone nonplussed is perplexed, unable to think anymore.

By the late twentieth century, *nonplussed* also came to mean almost the exact opposite—"*not* perplexed, *not* confounded, unfazed, calm." This opposite meaning of *nonplussed* may soon win the meanings race. Even Harvard-educated former President Obama used it in this way. We prefer to stick with the old definitions, but in the interests of not confusing others, we don't say *nonplussed* much. And you know, we're not nonplussed about that.

nonplussed (adj): perplexed

notoriety

"His notoriety in the sports medicine world and his passion for sports also earned him the position of team physician at the University of San Francisco, San Francisco State University, and Skyline College."

—PACIFIC HEIGHTS SURGERY CENTER WEBSITE

Who wants a notorious team physician? *Notoriety*'s basic meaning is "to be known (or notorious) for bad qualities," as in "Sweeney Todd, the demon barber of Fleet Street, achieved notoriety for his surgical crimes." (Note: Barber surgeons like the fictional Todd used to perform minor surgery in Victorian England, but Todd carried his duties overenthusiastically to include throat slitting.) To avoid negative connotations like this, you shouldn't use *notoriety* or *notorious* to describe anyone whose services you wish to advertise, and certainly not for surgeons.

Yes, *notoriety* can indeed also be used in a positive sense of being well known. But importantly, it usually isn't. Its association with its often evil adjective, *notorious*, gives it a certain lingering bad smell, so *notoriety* is best avoided when talking about friends or prominent people, unless you're referring to prominent criminals or incompetents. We suggest substituting positive synonyms like *renown*, *fame*, or *celebrity*.

Notoriety probably crossed over from France into England in the late 1500s, as the French word *notoriete*. But don't blame the French; they got it from the Medieval Latin *notorietatem*. *Notorious* is an earlier immigrant—it came into English from Latin in the 1200s or 1300s. *Notorious* originally meant "well known," but it so often hung out with derogatory nouns that it, along with *notoriety*, now tends to have a negative meaning. Just like Mom said in an old 1950s teen movie: Hang out with a bad crowd, and pretty soon your reputation is ruined.

notoriety (n): famous for negative qualities

obviate

"There are a number of works that might help you develop
your take on the Ariadne and Theseus myth (apologies for
obviating the obvious). . . ."

—PROFESSOR'S COMMENTS ON COURSEWORK POSTED ON
SKIDMORE COLLEGE'S WIKI

The good professor apparently wants to apologize for making
obvious something obvious. Instead he should be apologizing
for that "obviating."

Many people think *obviate* means "to make obvious," probably
because it also starts with the not-terribly-common *obv*. But
while they come from the same Latin root, *obvius*, they don't
mean the same thing. While *obvious* refers to something clear or
easy to understand, *obviate* means "to do away with, to render
unnecessary." The thing being obviated is something you don't
want happening, as in this 1567 use published in the *Register of the
Privy Council of Scotland*: ". . . to obviat and resist the effectis of . . .
wicked spitches and trevellis. . . ." (Yes, we, too, find that *spitches*
most interesting.)

Nowadays, *obviate* is commonly used in the phrase "obviate
the need," which is often sneered at by grammar nitpickers. If
obviate means "to make unnecessary," the phrase is redundant,
right? (Hint: This is a trick question.)

Those who say it's redundant are actually basing their
argument on incomplete data. They are focusing only on the
"to make unnecessary" meaning (which, in fairness, is the only
definition in a few dictionaries). But since *obviate* can also
mean "to anticipate and prevent the necessity (from arising),"

"obviate the need" isn't a redundancy at all. Grammarian Alexander Bain used the phrase himself in his 1879 *A Higher English Grammar*: "Certain pronouns also, as will presently be seen, obviate the necessity of repeating the great substitutes of the Noun in composition." And we think his thumbs-up obviates the need to go on any further.

obviate (v): to do away with, to make unnecessary

---

opportunistic / opportune

"It is a great and opportunistic time to be a disciple of Jesus Christ."

—CHURCH BULLETIN

Opportunistic used in the context of religious worship is, shall we say, an unfortunate usage? Try typing *opportunistic* in Google and you'll come up with a host of pejoratives associated with the word: "opportunistic infections," "opportunistic pathogens," "opportunistic bankers," and this from the *Winnipeg Sun* about a 1960s-era drug-infused celebrity: "Tommy comes across as an opportunistic slimeball who uses his looks and his upper-crust accent to get whatever he wants." (Note: We found "opportunistic slimeballs" cited frequently—many, as you might expect, with political, celebrity, or banking connotations.) So *opportunistic* is clearly not a word one would wish to associate with a religious institution, unless one is a militant and especially virulent atheist. *Opportune*, however, means "a time well chosen, appropriate" and is clearly the idea this house of worship was trying to get across.

Opportune has an interesting seafaring past. It comes from the Latin words *ob-* (toward) and *portus* (harbor), and describes a favorable wind pushing a ship home to its port. *Opportunistic* has similar earlier origins, but veered toward the bad in the 1870s, when Italian political parties used the word (in its Italian form) first to mean "taking advantage of circumstances," then in the sense of not caring about the morality of doing this. A useful political word. It was quickly picked up throughout Western Europe as a happy way of denigrating and abusing the opposing political party, a favorite pastime among self-satisfied speechifying statesmen: "Those guys are opportunistic, self-serving politicians, whereas we only care for the people."

opportunistic (adj): taking advantage of circumstances without regard to ethics

opportune (adj): appropriate or well-chosen time

ordinance / ordnance

"Marine Corps Quantico Explosive Ordinance Disposal"

—SIGN AT MILITARY BASE, EPISODE OF TV SERIES *NCIS*

According to what is written above, the *NCIS* marines keep busy disposing of explosive city laws. Not exactly exciting TV, but, then again, some city laws are pretty destructive.

Ordinance means "a governmental law, usually on the municipal or county level," as in "There's an ordinance against jaywalking in our town." The *NCIS* sign should have read "ordnance disposal." *Ordnance* is a collective noun meaning "military supplies (artillery, vehicles, ammunition, etc.)" or "the branch of the military dealing with these items." Disposing of them is a reasonable thing for these fictional marines to spend time doing. In the United Kingdom, the term *ordnance* is commonly used for all types of military supplies, while in the United States it is often used in a more restrictive sense to mean just missiles and bombs. So be especially careful going into a US ordnance disposal area—they're probably not just getting rid of old computer monitors.

The opposite error of using *ordnance* where *ordinance* should be is quite common as well: do a quick search online and it's easy to find talk about "city ordnances." We doubt the writers were talking about small town artillery, although these days you never know.

Confusing the two words is easy. It's even defensible etymologically. Both words come from the Latin word *ordinare* (to put into order). In one case, it's explosives, and in the other, it's city rules and regulations. But short of ordinances relating to ordnance, the two words remain far apart in usage, especially given their sometimes explosive differences.

ordinance (n): government law, usually county or municipal
ordnance (n): military supplies, usually explosive

---

panacea

"Two thousand years ago Greek scientists deemed *Aloe vera* the 'universal panacea.'"

—REALFARMACY WEBSITE

The ancient Greeks probably never deemed aloe vera a "universal panacea" because they presumably spoke ancient Greek well enough to know that the *pan* in *panacea* means "all," and the *acea* (*akos* in ancient Greek) means "remedy or cure." So *panacea* already means "universal cure." Chucking in the adjective *universal*, as in "universal panacea" means "universal universal cure," which is a teeny (or as the Greeks might say, *mikros*) bit redundant. (In fact, it's a bilingual tautology—from the ancient Greek *tauto*, meaning "same," and *logos*, meaning "word"—that is, same word or meaning used twice).

Another common and related mistake with *panacea* is to apply it as one cure for one specific disease or ailment—in other words, a partial panacea. A partial universal cure doesn't make much sense, nor does this sentence from the *Guardian*: "Meanwhile, after the ERM, the next supposed panacea for British inflation was central bank independence." That's a cure-all for only one thing, which is incorrect.

However, some authors (but few dictionaries) feel *panacea* can be used to mean a cure for an exceptionally complex problem, or a fairly large number of problems. Trotting this explanation out is always a good defense if someone accuses you of using *panacea* incorrectly. But in general, reserve *panacea* as a general cure for *all* (or at least a resoundingly large number of) illnesses, ailments, or problems. So we won't even begin to suggest that this book is a panacea for all your grammar problems.

panacea (n): cure-all

pandemic / epidemic / endemic

Hollywood and Bollywood love pandemic movies. *Contagion, I Am Legend,* and, yes, *Pandemic* all involve pandemics. So what's wrong with the CNN article above?

It should have said *epidemic,* not *pandemic.* There's a difference. *Pandemic* sounds more frightening, and it should. It comes from the ancient Greek *pan* (all) and *demos* (people), or in other words, a "worldwide epidemic affecting all (or at least a lot of) people."

Technically speaking, scientists rate different levels of contagious disease outbreaks. First, there's an *outbreak,* the sudden occurrence of a new disease or a much higher level of a known disease, in a relatively small area. (And yes, there's a film *Outbreak,* too). Then there's an *epidemic,* when the disease has spread to more than one community or country (and a film *Epidemic*). Finally, there's a *pandemic,* when the disease has spread worldwide or over a large area. The Black Death, or bubonic plague, is one of the best known of pandemics, killing millions of people in Asia and Europe. The World Health Organization has a more technical series of disease-spreading levels—from phase 1, where the disease is found only in animals, all the way to the pandemic phase 6.

The related word *endemic* comes from the ancient Greek *en-* (in) and *demos* (people), and means "particular to, found among a group." It doesn't have to refer to disease—for example, raccoons are endemic to North America, and pandemic (and epidemic) movies aren't endemic only to Hollywood.

pandemic (n): worldwide epidemic
epidemic (n): large outbreak of a disease
endemic (adj): prevalent in a certain group

---

parameter

"Sindh Governor Muhammad Zubair on Friday said that Karachi was the economic hub and a parameter of prosperity in the country."

—*THE NATION*

It has gotten to the point that you stumble upon parameters all over the place, including where they shouldn't be. *Parameter* is one of those words that has become overused probably because it seems so science-cool . . . even though it's often used humanities-wrong.

The problem is, *parameter* began as a mathematical term—meaning "an arbitrary constant or an independent variable"—which doesn't mean much to nonmathematicians. Even the supposedly nontechnical definition can be quite confusing: "a set of facts or a fixed limit that establishes or limits how something can or must happen or be done, as in: The researchers must keep within the parameters of the experiment" (*Cambridge Dictionary*). No wonder people aren't quite sure how to use it. But don't blame them for trying. It's okay (if slightly frowned upon) to use *parameter* to mean a metaphorical, not physical, boundary or limit, almost as a synonym for its near-twin *perimeter*. But people also use it to mean an individual element, example, or characteristic, and that's still not okay.

Harvard linguist Steven Pinker cites it as one of the most misused words in English. The *OED* says politely that "non-technical uses of parameter have attracted adverse comment from usage guides in the later 20th cent.," and the *American Heritage Dictionary* notes that in 1988, 88 percent of its usage panel gave a thumbs-down to *parameter* used to mean "characteristic," and 77 percent still rejected it in 2004, "suggesting that familiarity has not bred tolerance of this usage."

parameter (n): technically, an arbitrary constant or an independent variable; also used to denote a metaphorical boundary

---

pejorative

"Alistair Cooke, a former British intelligence officer, argues in the *Guardian* that the word 'terrorist' is a perjorative term."

—HONEST REPORTING BLOG

We suspect Honest Reporting misquoted Cooke. The intelligence officer probably said "pejorative," unless he wasn't that intelligent. . . .

There's no *per* in *pejorative*, but many people don't know it. We found "perjorative" almost everywhere: in academic books (*Oxford Handbook of Political Ideologies*), best sellers (Marr's *A History of the World*), academic papers (Harvard Law School), prestigious magazines (*New Scientist*), letters to the editor (*The Economist*), and in 62,000 (admittedly with many repeats) Benedict Cumberbatch–related fan and press discussions, mostly about what his fans call themselves and what he called others.

It's no surprise. As a copy editor on Copyediting.com noted, it's instinctive to put the *r* in: "When I type pejorative, I must consciously stop my left forefinger from dropping down on the *r* key after my middle finger taps the *e*. When I hear it spoken, it's often unclear whether there is an *r* sound at the end of the first syllable." There isn't.

Pejorative comes from the Latin word for "worse," *peior* (*i* and *j* were the same in Latin). But *pej* is an odd sound. (*Pejorative* and its cousins *pejorate, pejoration,* and *pejoratively* are the only *pej* words in English.) Contrast this with upward of one thousand *per* words. Another problem is that *pejorative* seems like it's related to *perjury*. It's not; *perjury* comes from two Latin words *per* (meaning, in this case, to ill effect) and *jurare* (to swear), which together mean "to swear falsely." So if you defend Benedict Cumberbatch online, take out the *r* and write *pejorative*.

pejorative (adj): disparaging; (n): a derogatory statement

---

penultimate / ultimate

"[Producer Steven Spielberg was] determined to find an actor from across the pond to play the penultimate American president."

—HUFFINGTON POST STORY ABOUT A PLANNED FILM BIOPIC ABOUT ABRAHAM LINCOLN

We don't think HuffPo meant to say Lincoln was the second-to-last American president in history, but that's just what they said . . . because *penultimate* means "second to last." But to many of us, *penultimate* sounds like it's the ultimate in ultimateness. People, organizations, and the media often get it wrong, especially when they're trying hard to sound erudite, since *penultimate* isn't one of those run-of-the-mill words one typically slips into conversation. So we get glaring errors like this in a program for the San Francisco Symphony: "All the otherworldly ability that Mozart possessed was brought to bear in the *Jupiter Symphony*, the final—and perhaps penultimate—symphony he produced." (Perhaps the symphony knows something quantum mechanical about Mozart that we don't know. . . .)

Maybe the symphony writers should have taken some Latin. *Penultimate* comes from two Latin words, *paene* (almost) and *ultima* (last). If you've ever taken Greek or Latin, you have probably run across it referring to the next-to-last syllable of a word. Modern Spanish and Portuguese use its cousin *penúltimo* in everyday conversation, but we don't. Well, except when we want to sound more educated—which is when we ultimately make mistakes.

And speaking of *ultimate,* if you really want to irritate people, there's this ultimate "ultimate" word: *preantepenultimate*, which means the *fifth* from the last. Linguists indubitably use this word to indicate words that are stressed on the fifth from the last syllable—such as, well, indubitably.

penultimate (adj): second from the last
ultimate (adj): last; (n) the final point

penumbra

"It also felt in keeping with the media circus that has emerged out of Trump's arrival in Washington, where a penumbra of reality television seems to hang over everything."

—YAHOO MOVIES/*HOLLYWOOD REPORTER*

Penumbra is one of those words that people use even though they are not entirely sure of its meaning. It's a pity, because *penumbra* is also one of those words that conveys a very evocative and specific image—when it is used properly.

But improper penumbras abound. We read of a "penumbra of things" or a "penumbra of options," even though a penumbra has nothing to do with quantity. Yes, there is a growing trend to use *penumbra* in place of *plethora*, perhaps because they both start with *p* and end with *a*. Even more common is using *penumbra* as a highfalutin way of saying "dark or shadowed." This is quasi-correct, as it does have something to do with shadows. But a *penumbra* isn't just any shadow; it's a quasi shadow.

The word was coined by astronomer Johannes Kepler in 1604 from the Latin *paene* (almost) and *umbra* (shadow) to describe the partial shadow around the darker shadow of an eclipse. Its meaning has extended outside of astronomy, with the concept of that partial shadow or aura applied figuratively to mean a hint of something undesirable, a periphery, the gray area between black and white concepts or ideas, and, similarly, in law, a right that is implied by an actual right or law, but isn't concrete or spelled out. The key in all of these is the notion of something partial. In case you're curious, the term *to take umbrage* (to take offense) also comes from the original total (not partial) *umbra* since it means "suspicion that someone has been slighted," i.e., under a shadow.

penumbra (n): partial shadow

---

perpetuate / perpetrate

"Watch Katie Couric Perpetuate a Fraud"

—HEADLINE, BEFORE IT'S NEWS

No, let's watch Katie Couric *perpetrate* a fraud. (Author's note: We don't think journalist Couric did.) To *perpetuate* is "to prolong something, to sustain." But the video and underlying text to the headline merely show Couric allegedly doing a one-time fraudulent broadcast. So she didn't keep the fraud going, she began it, and so she didn't perpetuate anything, she *perpetrated* it. (Not to perpetuate this, but we really don't think she perpetrated anything.)

Perpetrate means "to carry out an action, usually bad, or commit a crime or deception." We all know the related noun *perpetrator*, or its shortened form *perp*, from TV cop shows.

It's easy to confuse the two words, but their meanings are quite different. *Perpetrate* comes from two Latin words: *per* (completely) and *patrare* (to carry out). By the time it got to English, it had negative connotations it didn't have in the original Latin. *Perpetuate* comes from another old Latin word, *perpetuus* (an unbroken expanse, or continuing throughout). The distinctions can sometimes be confusing in use. For example, on the FBI website: ". . . Stanford perpetuated his fraud by paying bribes from a Swiss slush fund at Societe

Generale. . . ." We wondered: Did the FBI, the king of catching perpetrators, incorrectly use *perpetuated*? Or did they mean the perp prolonged the fraud through bribery? In reading the entire article, we think the FBI use was correct: the perpetrator perpetuated the fraud, but not in the indefinite sense of the word—the FBI got their man in the end.

perpetuate (v): to prolong something
perpetrate (v): to carry out a (usually bad) action, to commit a crime or deception

---

perquisite / prerequisite

"Multivariate calculus and linear algebra are perquisites for the course and it is assumed that students are familiar with the material."

—ECONOMICS 700: QUANTITATIVE METHODS IN ECONOMICS, UNIVERSITY OF NORTH CAROLINA COURSE CATALOG (FALL 2013)

We never took multivariate calculus, but we did take English and we know that instead of *perquisites*, the prof should have written *prerequisites*. It's an easy mistake to make (and the prof did use it correctly elsewhere), especially if your brain is dulled after going through reams of economic data.

A *prerequisite* is "a thing that is required as a prior condition" (as in multivariate calculus for Econ 700). A *perquisite*, or *perk* for short, is something that you get in addition to your normal job salary, usually a noncash benefit like use of a company car or jet. The two words are often confused, sometimes in the opposite sense, as in this from an accounting textbook: "Analyzing director . . . provisions as if they were salary, company cars or other personal corporate prerequisites simply makes no sense." No, that makes no sense. It should be *perquisites*.

The key to remembering the differences lies in the Latin-derived prefixes. *Prerequisite* has prefix *pre-* (before), as in preschool, so obviously *prerequisite* has to do with something before. *Perquisite* has prefix *per* (through) with the root word *quaere* (to seek). In Latin, *perquisitum* meant "a thing sought after," later "a thing gained." It came into English to mean "property acquired other than by inheritance." From there came the meaning of benefit that we have today. So we can say a prerequisite for perquisites is a good education. Remember that on a long afternoon in Econ 700.

perquisite (n): something extra (usually noncash) given in addition to the normal salary
prerequisite (n): something required as a prior condition

---

per se

"There's been a considerable amount of press on deconflicting the US and Russia. And I think that will continue, even though Russia has called it off, per se."

—RETIRED ADMIRAL MIKE MULLEN, FORMER CHAIRMAN OF THE JOINT CHIEFS OF STAFF ON *PBS NEWSHOUR*

With all due respect to Admiral Mullen, that "per se" should be called off as well. He has fallen into the trap of using *per se* indiscriminately and incorrectly. It has become very common to use it as a stand-in for "exactly," "sort of," or even as an ostensibly erudite "you know."

Per se doesn't mean any of those things. It means "intrinsically, in and of itself," or, more literally, "by or of itself." It is a Latin phrase formed of *per* (by or through) and *se* (itself), and is often (correctly) used to make a distinction between an element of something, and the larger thing itself, as in the inarguable 1853 example cited by the *OED*, "A pigstye in a city is per se a nuisance."

Interestingly, *per se* spawned the word *ampersand,* which was a corruption of the phrase "and per se." *Per se* entered English in the 1500s, and has consistently meant just what it always did, even though so many people persist in sprinkling it incorrectly in their conversation like a handful of croutons.

And don't get us started on an even more upsetting trend, the emergence of "per say." As if it's not enough that the term is misused, it's also misspelled. So we read sentences like this, from the popular website Hello Giggles: "Other notable moments included both President Dwight Eisenhower's 1953 inauguration parade, as well as President John F. Kennedy's 1961 inauguration parade—both of which showcased missiles and tanks (though they weren't technically "military parades," per say)."

Just say no.

per se (adv): intrinsically, in and of itself

perspective / prospective

"On Tuesday as many as ten jurors had been selected, however attorneys opted to bring in one hundred new perspective jurors to be screened."

—MSN LIFESTYLE WEBSITE, VIDEO STORY CAPTION ON TRIAL OF COMEDIAN BILL COSBY

Perspective jurors for a trial? Not likely. *Perspective* means basically two things: in art, "drawing on a two-dimensional surface to make something look three-dimensional," or in general, "a particular way of looking at or thinking about things," as in "We're writing this book from a grammatical perspective."

The word that MSN should have used is *prospective*, which means "expected in the future." A prospective juror, then, is someone who is expected to become a juror, which makes sense.

The differences between the two words arise from the prefixes. Both words share the same basic Latin root *specere* (to look at), but one has *per-* (through, in front, i.e., looking at closely or in a particular way), and the other has *pro-* (forward, in front, i.e., to look forward, look to the future).

"Perspective jurors" are frighteningly common where we wouldn't expect them—in legal documents. We found them in a handout sheet given to jurors by the National Association of Criminal Defense Lawyers, and even on a document by the US Federal Judicial Center—not exactly confidence building regarding their prospective handling of criminal cases. To be fair, this error seems to be more one of carelessness than not knowing the correct definition. But it's egregious just the same, particularly in a judicial context where precision may make the difference between being found guilty or not guilty. So, especially to legal writers, we say: Mind your pers and pros as well as your p's and q's. Case closed.

perspective (adj): making something look three-dimensional;
  (n): a particular way of looking at or thinking about things
prospective (adj): expected in the future

---

peruse

"I mean, they could have just casually perused the headlines."

—TWEET RESPONSE BY FORMER OBAMA SPEECHWRITER JON FAVREAU TO *WASHINGTON POST* TWEET ON RUSSIAN GOVERNMENT HACKERS, DNC FILES, AND STOLEN RESEARCH ON TRUMP

Since the preferred definition of *perused* means "to have examined carefully, with great attention to detail," the tweet above states that the Russians could have "just very carefully casually examined the headlines." Huh? What were those nefarious Russkies doing?

Thinking that *peruse* means "to read or examine quickly" or "to browse" instead of the opposite, "to fastidiously examine or read," is common. So common, in fact, that the formerly wrong definition is now formally acceptable even among such august authorities as those at the *OED*. They politely list it as a "later usage." So then, using *peruse* in that quick and dirty way isn't an error at all?

Weeeelll . . . we're not real fans of words having two opposite meanings. It makes things difficult. For example, when you said you perused my memo, did you read it thoroughly or just glance at it?

Speaking of not understanding what *peruse* means, it was first used to mean something quite different from either usage we've discussed—"to use up or wear out through use"—as in this ledger account of rope used in a voyage under the rule of Henry VII, cited in the *OED*: "Saile twyne . . . Spent & perused in a voiage into Lumbardye." When you think about it, you can see how "using up" came to mean paying careful attention or reading thoroughly. And now we've perused (using that archaic definition) all the space on this page for this word. However, you may peruse (either definition) what we've written at your leisure.

peruse (v): to read or examine closely

podium / lectern

"We can still hear his voice bellowing through the Senate chamber, face reddened, fist pounding the podium, a veritable force of nature, in support of health care or workers' rights or civil rights."

—PRESIDENT BARACK OBAMA IN HIS EULOGY FOR SENATOR TED KENNEDY

A *podium* is the raised platform where a speaker *stands* to deliver a speech, so Obama's vivid image of a red-faced Ted Kennedy in a Senate speech pounding the podium makes for a surprisingly gymnastic congressional session. Not to be outdone, Toronto mayor John Tory and Richard Nixon also had past episodes of podium pounding. Unless these men got on their hands and knees and started pounding away at the raised floor, we've got a linguistic conundrum. Or a bunch of pretty ridiculous (but flexible) men.

No, they didn't pound the podium, they pounded the *lectern*. That's the raised slanted stand where a speaker places notes for a speech. It seems almost everyone makes the mistake of confusing the two.

Podium comes from the Greek word *podion*, the diminutive of their word for foot, *pous*. (One of its modern English cousins is podiatrist, so logically a podium is where a speaker places his feet.) *Lectern* comes from the Medieval Latin words *lectrum* or *lectorium*, via the classical word *legere* (to read).

The key point is the lectern is the stand for your reading materials—it can be a tabletop version or a stand-alone. But you stand (or sit) behind a lectern; you stand *on* the podium. Once there, if you're so inclined, you can begin happily pounding the lectern in front of you. But inform any journalists in the audience you're pounding the lectern and not the podium. You wouldn't want to give their etymologically knowledgeable readers the wrong impression.

podium (n): raised platform where a speaker stands to make a speech
lectern (n): raised stand behind which a speaker sits or stands

---

practicable / practical

"Handmade Organic Soaps: for the practicable person on your list give a gift that's fresh!"

—NYC ANNEX MARKET'S GIFT GUIDE

A practical person might indeed want handmade soap (actually, an impractical person might too, but that's neither here nor there). But a practicable one? Well, that's problematic, because a person, practical or otherwise, can't be practicable.

Practicable and *practical* are often confused and for good reason. They come from the same root—the Latin *practica* (practice), from the Greek *praktike*—and are separated only by the insertion of an *ab*. (*Practicable* evolved from the Medieval Latin *practicabilis* (capable of being used), while *practical* evolved from the Medieval Latin *practicalis* (of or relating to practice or action). Not only do they look so similar, but there is a bit of an overlap in their meanings. *Practicable* is an adjective meaning "able to be put into practice," in other words, something that is feasible or possible. *Practical* has more meanings—among them "of or relating to practice," "useful," "suitable for a certain purpose," and "capable of being into effect," which seems a lot like *practicable*.

But there is a distinction. Something practicable isn't necessarily practical and vice versa. For example, trimming a hedge with a hedge trimmer is practical, but not practicable if you have no hedge trimmer. If, on the other hand—while we're not sure why you'd do it—you have nail scissors, it is practicable to trim your hedge with them, but definitely isn't practical. We can only hope you have a lot of time on your hands.

practicable (adj): able to be put into practice
practical (adj): useful, suitable

TO WHOM IT MAY CONCERN, OR WHO'S ON FIRST: THE WHO/WHOM CONUNDRUM

Most people avoid using "whom" because they think it sounds, well, like you have a stick up your butt. There's something overly correct about it. But there is a time and place for whom, at least for purists. (Note: This is one case where we tend to side with the purists, although we concede that there is a lot of truth in that stick issue.)

When to whom and when to who? It's really not tough. You use *who* as a subject, and *whom* as an object, indirect or direct. An indirect object use of whom goes like this: "To whom am I speaking?" ("Who am I speaking to" is technically wrong, although we violate our own rule and say it ourselves.) A direct object use goes like this: "He hit whom?" Who works when you would use he, she, or they; whom with him, her, them. If you aren't sure, just replace the who/whom with he or him: "Who/whom called me?" "He called me," not "him called me."

But avoiding "whom" is common nowadays. For example, Infographic recently had a graphic: "Who had sex with who on *Game of Thrones*." We don't know the answer, but the question should have been "who had sex with whom" since "she had sex with he" is definitely wrong. Similarly, Twitter has a little box at the top of the screen saying "Who to follow." You wouldn't follow she, you'd follow her . . . so it should be "Whom." Presumably, Twitter is a little too casual for that correct "whom."

Let us close with a particularly dreadful joke:
Knock knock.
Who's there?
To.
To who?
It's to whom!
We'd like to thank whomever actually laughed at that.

prescribe / proscribe

"Bar Steward Duties:

SET UP AND TEAR DOWN OF BARS FOR FUNCTIONS

Monitor stock supplies to ensure full bar available at all times, within proscribed limits."

—HELP WANTED AD FOR THE HAMILTON GOLF AND COUNTRY CLUB (ANCASTER, ONTARIO)

Proscribe means "to forbid, or denounce." So according to Hamilton Golf and Country Club, their bartender must ensure a full supply of booze within forbidden limits. That's one tough job description. The word should be *prescribed*, which means "to make a rule or beneficial recommendation" (or "to give a medical prescription," of course.)

Proscribed is often mistaken for *prescribed*. This example is only one among many, including one from an acclaimed grammarian. (Others have kindly said that was probably an error by the publisher, not the grammarian. We agree. In fact, we always blame publishers ourselves. Or editors.) The two words are very similar, except in definition. They share the same Latin root word *scribere* (to write). Even their two different prefixes, *pro-* and *prae-* (the *a* was lost over the years), both mean essentially the same thing: "before."

But while *prescribe* has a positive connotation, *proscribe* has an ominous past. At first, *proscribe*, in Latin, simply meant "to announce publicly," but under Roman dictator Sulla, it took on a skewed meaning: the posting of lists of people in the Forum who were enemies of the state (as helpfully decided by Dictator Sulla, natch). Proscribed people were stripped of

Roman citizenship, and citizens were invited to kill them for fun and profit.

Prescribe has kept a more benign meaning of "making a beneficial recommendation or orders, or making medical prescriptions"—which leads us to a clever *Reason* magazine headline, referring to doctors being prohibited from prescribing: "Prescription Proscription."

prescribe (v): to recommend or order something, often medical treatments

proscribe (v): to forbid or denounce

---

presumptive / presumptuous

"It would be presumptive of me to think I know the most important thing on people's minds."

—SENATOR CHUCK GRASSLEY, QUOTED IN THE *MUSCATINE* [IA] *JOURNAL*

No, it would be *presumptuous* of him to do that. *Presumptive* means "presumed, inferred, giving good grounds for belief," which wasn't what Senator Chuck was trying to say. He was humbly saying it would be overly bold (presumptuous) of him to claim that he knows what people are thinking.

The humble senator aside, saying *presumptive* to mean *presumptuous* is common but incorrect (even though the *OED* includes it as the third definition, along with examples from such notables as Robert Burns: "I was not so presumptive as to imagine that I could make verses like printed ones"). Auld Rabbie Burns aside, we think it's excessively presumptuous of the rest of us to blur definitions. The *American Heritage* Usage

Panel overwhelmingly agrees, with 83 percent surveyed saying *presumptive* should not be used to mean *presumptuous*.

The reverse mistake is also fairly common, as in this *Wired* magazine article: "Bruce Willis might still be John McClane, but his screen son and presumptuous heir to the franchise is manimal Jai Courtney. . . ." Unless the writer thinks Jai Courtney is arrogant, overly confident, and bold (a possibility, he's certainly been savaged by critics in the past), the correct word is *presumptive*.

Presumptive is often used for heirs apparent—literature abounds with presumptive heirs and heiresses to the thrones of Europe, but presumptuous heirs are rare, except in clever plays on words, as in this: "Although an heir-presumptive, Henry the Second is no presumptuous heir. He isn't talking, he's working as his father and grandfather did."

presumptive (adj): presumed
presumptuous (adj): overly bold

---

preternatural

"Whole Foods . . . is the largest supermarket in Manhattan. Milling about its preternaturally clean aisles and sculptured displays of produce, shoppers move pastorally slowly by New York standards."

—*GREENING THE RED, WHITE, AND BLUE: THE BOMB, BIG BUSINESS, AND CONSUMER RESISTANCE IN POSTWAR AMERICA*

Unless you think finding grass-fed beef steaks for $6.99 a pound is a paranormal event, going to Whole Foods isn't a supernatural experience. It seems kind of ordinary to us.

In fairness to the writer, he isn't (we hope) using *preternatural* in its preferred way—to mean "going beyond nature, supernatural"—but to mean "extraordinary."

And . . . there's a problem with that as well.

Let's start with looking at the original technical meaning of the word. *Preternatural* comes from the combination of two Latin words, *praeter* (beyond) and *naturalis* (natural). It's obviously very similar to *supernatural*, which has the prefix *super-* (above) rather than *preter*. Both words are fairly (the key word here is "fairly") interchangeable. Some persnickety types note that there's a distinction: *preternatural* means something we don't yet have an explanation for now but might have in the future, whereas *supernatural* means something that will never have a scientific explanation. If you've seen that horror classic *The Haunting* (the 1963 version, not the awful remake), you heard "preternatural" used in that sense by the scientific ghost hunter. But outside of Hollywood and Oxford, that distinction seems nitpicky. As for "extraordinary," while dictionaries include this as an acceptable meaning, why do you need it? To sound smart? We think that's preternaturally silly.

Bluntly put, *preternatural* seems a useless affectation in *both* of its uses. If something is supernatural, say it. If it's extraordinary, say that.

preternatural (adj): going beyond nature

prevaricate / procrastinate

> "For May, it mirrors the honeymoon that Gordon Brown enjoyed after taking over as Prime Minister—and the subsequent crash in poll ratings after he prevaricated over whether to hold an election."
>
> —*THE SPECTATOR* [UK]

Prevaricate means "to deviate from the truth, to avoid telling the truth by equivocation." Unless Prime Minister Gordon Brown was lying about whether to hold an election—you never know with politicians—he was *procrastinating*, which is the word the writer should have used. This error is surprisingly frequent, as is using *prevaricating* to mean "vacillating."

We're not going to prevaricate, vacillate, or procrastinate in telling the truth about the word. It has a wicked past. It comes from the Latin *praevaricatus* (to walk or plow crookedly). In medieval Europe, "praevaricators" were sinners or renegades. In Henry VIII's England, "prevaricators" were those who abandoned the queens he was planning to do away with by various creative means: "The King . . . licensed Queen Katherine to choose counsellors . . . some played the prevaricators, and fled from her to the King's side." Poor Katherine. At least she kept her head. Today *prevaricate* is most often used as a polite way of saying someone is lying by evading telling the truth rather than by fabricating falsehoods. *Equivocating*, when someone chooses words carefully, also describes lying by omission.

Now for a problem: Especially in the United Kingdom, *prevaricate* can be used in the sense of delaying or dilly-dallying.

The *Oxford English Dictionary* notes that this is probably due to confusion with *procrastinate*. All of their examples of this usage are English, as is the example here. But as ex-colonial Americans, we're going against the Queen's English and stick with our usage, and baby, we ain't prevaricating.

prevaricate (v): to avoid telling the truth
procrastinate (v): to defer, to delay

---

principal / principle

"Let's call it a big mistake, and it's one that illustrates the key principal of bad movie remakes: To really earn a place on the scroll of shame, a remake almost has to risk tarnishing the reputation of a movie we love."

—*VARIETY*

Yes, let's call it a big mistake indeed. That "principal," that is, which should be *principle*—unless, of course, the writer was referring to the key main person of bad movie remakes. (We suspect this isn't the case.)

This is another case of homophonic horror in which two words that sound alike get confused with each other. In this case, the two have absolutely nothing in common other than the sound.

Principle is a noun, meaning "rule, doctrine, standard." *Principal* is both an adjective and a noun. As an adjective, it means "chief, primary, most important"; as a noun, it refers to a person who plays a lead role or is in a high position, money on which interest is paid, or a school head. No overlap there.

There's virtually no overlap in their later etymology either. *Principle* entered English in the late fourteenth century from the Old French *principe* (origin, cause), from the Latin *principium* (origin). *Principal* also came from the Old French, but from *principal* (most important), from the Latin *principales* (most important, original) from *princeps* (first man, chief).

But the confusion between the two persists. In the latter case, it's particularly sad to see references in news stories to the "school principle." When we were kids, we were often told that the best way to remember how to spell *principal* was to think "the principal is your pal" (even if he or she wasn't). If a ten-year-old can grasp that concept, surely adults can too!

principal (adj): chief, primary; (n): lead person
principle (n): rule, doctrine

---

pristine

"It's time to join the gods when you enter into the most pristine bathroom you've ever seen."

—VEGAS WEBSITE

Okay, let's be honest: this is one of those usage examples that only the most committed grammarians would quibble about. We decided to include it because one of us was among the many who thought *pristine* referred to something spotlessly clean or absolutely perfect—like new, pure—and that was that. But that *isn't* that.

This is the most common meaning today, but *pristine* actually initially meant something different. It entered English in the 1530s, from the Latin *prīstinus*, meaning "former or previous" as well as "ancient and old." And that is just what it meant for several centuries—ancient, primitive, the original state. With this meaning, you could say "that filthy swamp is pristine" and be absolutely correct. Granted, you might get some odd looks.

It wasn't until 1899 that the familiar meaning of *pristine*, when referring to something natural (pure, unspoiled, or untouched), came into use. And it wasn't until even later that *pristine* began being applied to human-made objects that were spotless or as good as new. But super-sticklers will argue that this is a sloppy usage. The *OED* politely mentions that this sloppy usage of *pristine* is considered "ignorant" by educated speakers. Humph, say we. Feel free to boast about your pristine bathroom in your house by the pristine swamp, if you so wish.

pristine (adj): original; now also pure, spotless

---

prodigal

"President Obama in Kenya: Prodigal son returns—but can he bring much needed change to his father's homeland?"

—*THE INDEPENDENT*

Taking the preferred definition of *prodigal*, this headline can be rewritten as "President Obama in Kenya: Recklessly wasteful spendthrift son returns." Although we imagine a certain subset of the electorate would enthusiastically agree, we doubt the headline writer meant this. Ditto for a writer on "prodigal CEO" Steve Jobs of Apple.

For all too many of us, *prodigal* means "wandering," not the correct "wasteful." The problem is that most of us know the word from the famous New Testament parable of the Prodigal Son about the youngest of two sons "who set off for a distant country and there squandered his wealth in wild living" (Luke 15:13). For some reason, the going to distant parts took hold, the wild living didn't. There's no question about what the New Testament meant to say—in the original New Testament Greek, the adjective for the prodigal son was *asotos* (dissipated or debauched); the Latin translators used the Latin word *prodigus* (wasteful) and from there it came into English with the same meaning.

But today, *prodigal* meaning "wandering" has become so often used it's almost acceptable, although most dictionaries still frown on it, as do we. They don't frown, however, on using *prodigal* a bit more in a positive sense, meaning "lavish, luxuriant, especially abundant," as of a mouthwatering dessert: peach pie, with a hint of cinnamon and prodigal with whipped cream that melts into the warm fruit. And neither do we. Now let's eat.

prodigal (adj): wasteful

---

random

"The lullaby my husband puts our son to sleep with is so random. It's 'Don't Stop 'Til You Get Enough' by Michael Jackson."
—QUOTE IN *PEOPLE* MAGAZINE

Well, a lot of people *have* gotten enough! Of *random*, that is. . . . You can't escape it these days, particularly when attached to "so." "So random" is a popular Instagram tag and meme and, paired with an xD emoticon or a LOL, pops up on Tumblr, reddit, 4chan. But often what is so random is so wrong.

Random means "having no purpose or aim," and describes something that occurs without a pattern. It technically doesn't mean "unexpected," "arbitrary," "weird," or "funny," even though that's often how it is used nowadays.

When it first appeared in the fourteenth century, *random* was a noun meaning "great speed or impetuosity" and was spelled *randon*, probably an offspring of the German *randir* (to run fast). It became an adjective in the mid-1600s with the same meaning it currently has. But in the late 1960s, the new *random* emerged, primarily among computer geeks. A 1971 article in MIT student newspaper the *Tech,* cited by the OED, refers to students who were not part of their community as "randoms" and "randomized tools." From there, it appeared in the *Hacker's Dictionary* (which collected comp-sci speak in the 1980s) and began seeping into nontech areas (like 1995 movie *Clueless*, in which the Valley girls referred to things as "random"). In about 2004, "so random" emerged as the internet meme Katy t3h PeNgU1N oF d00m. And *so random* took off.

As for us, while we both think using *random* randomly is wrong, we must admit that one of us actually does use it in spite of herself. That's so random!

random (adj): having no purpose or no pattern

redundant

"[The appendix] has long been regarded as a potentially troublesome, redundant organ, but American researchers say they have discovered the true function of the appendix."

—ABC NEWS ONLINE

Whatever you think about human appendices (and they probably don't enter into your thoughts very much), we can confidently tell you they're not redundant and that this ABC News article statement is technically wrong. Why? Because we've got only one appendix each, and *redundant* means "an excess of something."

But wait, says a hypothetical, clever dictionary looker-upper, can't *redundant* also mean an excess of something in another way, as in "superfluous to one's needs"? Yes, so here ABC News *could* be correct, but not if you go on to read the article (which we've very kindly done for you). ABC says until recently, the appendix had no known function and was regarded as completely useless. So ABC News couldn't be suggesting that it was an "excess of something in terms of one's needs," since they thought it wasn't needed at all. Not to be redundant in pointing this out, but ABC was wrong in using the word according to either basic definition.

The origin of *redundant* helps solidify the definition. It came from the Latin *redundantem*, *re-* (again) and *unda* (wave), which combined means "rising over and above in waves, overflowing." Picture filling a glass with too much milk and, as it flows over the top, you've got milk redundancy . . . and a messy kitchen floor. And now here's a famous redundant news report: "The robbery was committed by a pair of identical twins. Both are said to be aged about 20."

redundant (adj): more than enough, an excess

---

refute

"During the late 1940s, Jackson Pollock's radical approach to painting revolutionized what it meant to create art. By dripping, flinging, and spattering paint onto his canvas laid onto the floor, he refuted centuries of tradition."

—ART GALLERY OF ONTARIO (AGO) WEBSITE

By spattering paint onto a canvas, Jackson Pollock wasn't proving centuries of tradition wrong. Instead, Jackson was *repudiating* tradition, which is "to refuse to accept or be associated with." Whatever you think of Pollock's art (half of us don't like it), we both unanimously admit it doesn't look at all similar to traditional works by Rembrandt or Monet. It clearly repudiates those old styles, but it doesn't prove anything.

That's *refute*'s job. *Refute* means "to prove a person or statement wrong with evidence and arguments." A lawyer refutes charges in court by presenting evidence convincing a judge and jury. Using *refute* to mean *repudiate* is generally not acceptable in the Court of Good English. The *American Heritage* Usage Panel said they have "scant affection for this usage," with 89 percent coming out against it.

However, there's another common (mis)usage of *refute* that is ever increasingly becoming acceptable, even though according to the *American Heritage Dictionary* it's generally regarded as "incorrect or inappropriate," and we agree. This is to substitute *refute* for "to deny the accuracy of," as in "The senator categorically refuted the charges of malfeasance but declined to go into details." While we're at it about charges and protestations of innocence, don't forget *rebut*—"to oppose by using evidence but not yet actually proving it." There's actually a hierarchy of words regarding legal charges: Someone first *denies* a charge, then *rebuts* by using evidence, and then *refutes* it (i.e., wins or convinces) by successfully proving it via evidence. Case dismissed!

refute (v): to prove someone or something wrong using evidence and/or arguments

---

regime / regimen

"It is best when used regularly, as part of your morning skincare regime."

—*VOGUE* [UK]

If you are like us, you learned that *regimen* is the word for "a course of action to improve one's health or well-being." So you would see an example like the above and think *regime* is wrong. After all, a *regime* is a government and has nothing to do with taking your vitamins. Right?

As you have probably guessed, this is a bit of a trick question. Yes, a *regimen* is "a program you follow." And a *regime* is most often used to mean "a government or administration," particularly in a negative way (a fascist regime, a heavy-handed regime). But like *regimen*, *regime* also means "course of action." This isn't a recent development. The *OED* notes that *regime*'s first meaning in 1314 was "medical treatment," and the notion of government came about in about 1350. So there is a definite precedent for *regime* being used interchangeably with *regimen*. *Regime* reigns supreme in British English where *regimen* is rarely used, while in American English *regimen* is still used more often in health contexts. (Note: You can also see a fairly healthy smattering of diet and vitamin "regiments," which is definitely unhealthy word usage!) A quick check of Google shows that *regime* is most often preceded by words like "authoritarian," "fascist," and "military," while *regimen* is preceded by "diet," "exercise," and "health." But as Fowler's *A Dictionary of Modern English Usage* notes, even doctors use *regime* these days.

So, yes, it appears that the days of regimen-only are over . . . in what you could call a linguistic regime change.

regime (n): a government or administration (particularly in a negative way); regimen
regimen (n): rules or proscribed actions about diet or health

---

restive / restful

"Here in Siouxland it might be a restive day at the fishin' hole or a contemplative walk at Bacon Creek."
—*SIOUX CITY* [SD] *JOURNAL*

A *restive* day at the fishing hole could mean a strange day of fishing—fidgeting and maybe even straining at restraints, chains, ropes, or controls imposed by outside authorities—maybe more of a BDSM day and not exactly our idea of a peaceful fun time in Siouxland. The writer presumably meant a "restful" day at the fishin' hole, to go alongside that contemplative walk at Bacon Creek.

Restive looks restful, but it isn't by a long shot. In fact, you might say that *restive* means almost the exact opposite of *restful*, even though it doesn't look that way. *Restive* comes from the Latin verb *restare* (to remain), and originally meant "inclined to remain still," which indeed can be quite restful.

But then came the idea of *making* something (usually a horse) remain still, and from there came the idea of a fidgety horse not wanting to remain still but being forced to, and from there we have today's meaning of *restive* as "difficult to control, nervous, restless," often with the idea of being externally restrained. *Restless*, a similar word, means "restive without any external restraint," but nowadays both words are relatively synonymous. Still, it's best to maintain the helpful distinction between the two. For example, if you say you had a restive night sleeping with your partner, your friendly neighborhood grammarian might think certain things about your bedtime practices you'd rather not broadcast.

restive (adj): difficult to control, restless
restful (adj): gives a feeling of calm and relaxation

reticent / reluctant

"Investors reticent to buy pricy US 2Y Treasuries"
—HEADLINE, REUTERS

In the example above, "reticent" is being used to mean "reluctant." *Reticent* means "quiet, shy, disinclined to speak." The article isn't saying investors are not inclined to speak about two-year Treasury notes, it's saying they're not wild about buying them (and who can blame them with low interest rates and high prices). So is the headline wrong?

Well, nowadays many say no, although grammar purists shout an emphatic yes. *Reticent* originally meant pretty much *only* "keeping silent." Its origins from the Latin clearly show this: *re-tacere* (to keep silent.) *Reluctant* comes from the Latin *re-luctare* (to struggle against). In both cases, the prefix *re-* reinforces the meaning of the verb.

Reticent came late into English, probably sometime in the 1800s. After a hundred years or so, it became acceptable to attach a "to" or "about" to *reticent* and use it to mean "hesitant or reluctant *to talk* about something," which makes some sense. If you're reluctant to buy something, you're probably also disinclined to speak about it. From there, *reticent* expanded into a general meaning of *reluctant*. Many grammarians accept the former (mis)usage of *reticent* to mean "being reluctant to talk about something," but they feel that taking it one step further to mean "being reluctant about anything" is too much. In fact, we won't remain reticent; we are not reluctant to say, keep 'em separate!

reticent (adj): not inclined to speak
reluctant (adj): hesitant, unwilling

revert

When we first read this sentence, we almost laughed. Someone promising resume help who can't even use "revert" correctly? Turns out the joke was on us.

True, in most dictionaries, *revert* does not mean "reply" or "return." It means "to return to an original state or to return to the original owner." Correctly, you can say, "The money reverts to me," but you should not say, "Revert to me soonest."

Well, at least in these parts. Ben Zinner in a *New York Times* article noted, "unbeknownst to most dictionaries, *revert* has been leading another life in several varieties of world English, notably the kind spoken on the Indian subcontinent." There, it *is* commonly also used to mean "reply." It's gotten such status that even the *OED* now lists this definition as correct (and what word could want higher praise than that?), although essentially confined to India. But since India is the world's second-largest English-speaking country (125 million currently, expected to quadruple in ten years), that's a lot of people using *revert* to mean "reply."

So what should we do? As one blogger on a language blog said, "As long as u use 'revert' in India for 'reply,' it's 100% correct!! . . . ;-)." We agree. ;-) Likewise, here on the other side of the globe, u should do as we do and revert to the original definitions.

revert (v): to return to an original state or to return to the original owner

scarify

"Those early recordings—1981's *Fire of Love* and 1982's *Miami*—are now considered classic LA albums that fuse together the Dionysian mythologies of Jim Morrison, Iggy Pop, and Darby Crash with the corny faux-traditionalism and pop hooks of Creedence Clearwater Revival, topped off by the scarifying, blood-curling [sic] imprecations of Robert Johnson and Howlin' Wolf."

—*LA WEEKLY*

We are among the first to admit we love albums that fuse together Dionysian mythologies with faux-traditionalism. But we draw the line at scarifying imprecations. And, frankly, we're not convinced that rock vocals can scar one.

Scarifying doesn't really mean "scary." It actually means "to make scratches or incisions" (as in the skin, like the body mod technique of scarifying) or "to break up the surface of something" (like a road). It entered English in the fifteenth century from the Middle French *scarifier* (score), which evolved from the Greek *skariphasthai* (to scratch an outline), which initially came from the word for "sketch," *skariphos*. But there was and has been nothing about the word connected with scaring.

Still people persist in believing that *scarify* is a fancy "scary." Thus we wind up reading about internet message boards that are "pretty scarifying" and the like. This is a sign of the times, of English changing as people get sloppier with the language, right? Uh, no, actually it's wrong. There is a precedent for this. The *OED* lists a second entry for *scarify*, from the slang, with an irregular (i.e., not "right") meaning "to scare." Unlike *scarify*'s etymological background, this *scarify* comes from adding an *-ify* suffix to the word *scare*. And it first appeared in print back in 1794. That said, though, old doesn't make it better. So when we see Darth Vader being referred to as "arguably the most compellingly scarifying villain in filmdom," as the *Spokesman-Review* [Spokane, WA] did, we should still find it scary.

scarify (v): to make scratches or incisions (as in the skin); to break up the surface of something (like a road)

---

simplistic

"Even though IKEA gets looked down on by many people, IKEA has many items that are bargains. Not only does it offer affordable and simplistic solutions to home décor and furnishings. . . ."

—LIVING GREEN AND FRUGALLY WEBSITE

Here's a simple but not simplistic rule of thumb: *simple* = good, *simplistic* = bad. Well, okay, it's really not as simple as that, but almost.

Simplistic means "characterized by a great deal of simplicity"—which sounds good, but it almost always means too much simplicity, a plethora of simplicity, as in an overly simple solution to a complex problem. The writer of the example above was not trying to disparage IKEA home furnishings, but to say they give easy and *simple* solutions to home decor.

How *simplistic* came to mean "overly simple" is lost to history. According to some sources, it originally merely meant "simple," but at least as far back as 1867, it took on its negative meaning.

(There's also an archaic meaning of *simplistic* having to do with simple, or medicinal, herbs, but that usage is long gone.)

One word of warning: Never modify *simplistic* with "overly" or similar words. Since *simplistic* already means overly simple, saying something is "overly simplistic" means something is "overly overly simple" and that is a clear tautology. Of course, that doesn't mean it's not all over the place, such as this recent utterance by Apple CEO Tim Cook: "That is overly simplistic, and it is not true."

simplistic (adj): characterized by much simplicity, usually in a negative sense

---

stanch / staunch

". . . and unless we staunch the wound the haemorrhage of humanity will continue."

—BRITISH FOREIGN SECRETARY BORIS JOHNSON IN THE *SPECTATOR* [UK]

Seeing "staunch the wound" become the norm makes us need to stanch our tears. Yes, *stanch*. It's a word that has fallen out of popularity lately as *staunch* takes its place. But we stand staunchly behind stanch, dang it. And now that we've gotten that out of our system. . . .

Stanch is a verb meaning "to stop the flow of blood or other bodily emissions" and, traditionally, *staunch* is an adjective meaning "loyal, steadfast." But *staunch* is now often used as a verb, too . . . meaning "to stop the flow of blood."

It is easy to see why *staunch* stands in so often for *stanch*. There is only a *u* separating them, for one thing. Even more confusingly, "staunch" is a spelling variation for the verb *stanch* and "stanch" for the adjective *staunch*. That said, it's more common to spell it "staunch" when it's an adjective, and "stanch" when it's a verb.

But *staunch* as a verb is on the upswing. According to the Google Ngram Viewer, which charts usage of words and phrases in books, "staunch the flow" has been more often used than the correct "stanch the flow" in recent years. They were neck and neck until about 1980 when *staunch* took the lead. And there it remains.

stanch (v): to stop the flow of bodily emissions, usually blood
staunch (adj): loyal, steadfast; (v): to stop the flow of bodily emissions

statistically significant

"Researchers found that, in general, Facebook is 'a positive, significant predictor of divorce rate and spousal troubles.' Of course, there are some limits to this finding . . . but the study's authors feel they're noticing something that's genuinely statistically significant."

—OZY

You see it all the time nowadays, particularly in health and wellness news stories like the above: A study has shown that Facebook might destroy your marriage! And the findings are— drumroll—statistically significant! Oh no—time to panic! But it might not be time to panic at all.

Scientists, statisticians, hypochondriacs, and in-the-know laypeople understand that *statistically significant* doesn't necessarily mean that the results were significant in the sense of "Wow!" It just means that they signify something, that whatever was observed has only a low probability that it was due to chance, so instead it is probably due to a systemic cause. You'll note that there is nothing there about importance or impact, implied or otherwise. The problem is, in nonstatistical use, *significant* means something noteworthy or important, something to make you sit up and take notice. So nonstatistical types see *statistically significant* and think it refers to something big. But it doesn't have to be. A study can find something statistically significant that has only a tiny effect. In other words, something statistically significant can actually be *in*significant. For example, Facebook could increase the risk of divorce by a statistically significant 1 percent. Big deal.

This is why many scientists wish the developer of statistical significance, British statistician R. A. Fisher, had called it something else. As mathematician Jordan Ellenberg says, " 'Statistically significant' is one of those phrases scientists would love to have a chance to take back and rename. . . . 'Statistically noticeable' or 'Statistically discernible' would be much better."

statistically significant (adj): refers to the mathematical probability that something didn't occur by chance

suspect / suspicious

"Asked about the situation this week, Niagara County Democratic Committee Chairman Daniel Rivera said he was suspicious of the fact that Cafarella and Legislator Jason Murgia—a Democrat who caucuses with Republicans—share the same treasurer. . . . 'That's why I'm suspect about the whole thing,' Rivera said."

—*NIAGARA GAZETTE* [NIAGARA FALLS, NY]

This *Niagara Gazette* article is particularly interesting because the newspaper correctly said that the politician was "suspicious" about something, whereas the politician himself incorrectly said he was "suspect" about something. *Suspect* cannot be used this way. We suspect the politician didn't realize that *suspicious* was the correct word.

Suspect is a busy word like many others. It can be a noun ("the suspect was arrested"), a verb ("I suspected him"), or an adjective ("the evidence was suspect"). But *suspect* absolutely cannot fill in for *suspicious* when you want to say that you or someone suspects a person or group and has feelings of suspicion. You never, ever have feelings of suspect; not that people aren't trying. We found numerous examples of people writing how they were "suspect" about husbands, wives, businesses, political parties, even about fraudulent footwear companies. In all cases, they were *suspicious* instead (often with good reason).

As you may suspect, *suspect* and *suspicious* come from Latin, combining two words *sub* (under) and *spicere* (look)— "looking from under." Both originally also had a meaning of "admire," but quickly got the meanings of "looking at secretly," and hence, the meanings we all know. And now, here's a short passage from great English poet Chaucer, who used both words correctly back in the 1380s: "Suspecious was the diffame of this man, Suspect his face, suspect his word also. Suspect the tyme in which he this began."

suspect (adj): untrustworthy; (n) one who is suspected (often of a crime); (v): to conjecture, to mistrust
suspicious (adj): distrustful, wary

tact / tack

"A New Tact in the MTS Fight"
—HEADLINE, *NY PRESS*

Tact means "the art or ability of saying things that are inoffensive." *Tack* means "a new course or direction." So in this case, the MTS fight was taking a new tack. (Maybe toward a more tactful dump truck arrangement? Nah.)

While *tack* has many other definitions (to attach, join, etc.), the area where it's most confused is in the sense of a changing of course. *Tack* initially was concerned with fastening, as it still is in sewing. By the late 1400s, it also came to mean specifically "the rope fastening the corner of a sail in place." It was just a short step (or knot) away to use *tack* in the sense of manipulating the sail ropes to turn course, and from there the technical sailing definition—"turn a ship's course toward the wind at an angle." And now, of course, it is used metaphorically without sails or wind to simply mean "changing course."

And speaking of changing course, we're going to: Never, ever tack in the direction of using "in tack" as a substitute for *intact*.

This appalling misuse is all over the place, especially on eBay, which is filled with descriptions of "in tack" book bindings, "in tack" car decals, and "in tack" Sega Genesis labels. The only area on eBay where *in* and *tack* may come together correctly seem to be the horse supply area—*tack* is also a term for equine equipment or horse accessories. But even here we found this sale: "Tack. Only been used a few time items still intack." Neigh!

tact (n): the art of saying inoffensive things
tack (n): new course or direction; (v) to fasten something down; in sailing, to change course

---

tendentious

"I would submit that they do not necessarily add incentive to the already tendentious struggle that playwrights face in trying to make a life in the theater."

—HUFFINGTON POST

In this article defending playwrights against critics, the author refers to their "tendentious struggle." We must take exception to this, even though as writers we're sympathetic to his point of view . . . which, in a neat segue (if we may say so ourselves), brings us to the correct definition of *tendentious*: "tending toward a particular point of view; often biased or partisan."

While our tendency is to agree with the writer's opinions, we say *tendentious* doesn't make much sense here. *Strenuous* or *toilsome* are better fits (and great ways to describe the hard life of writing. Ask us . . . if you have a few days).

The problem is that *tendentious* sounds like it means the preceding words. It's easy in the heat of the moment to chuck it in where it doesn't belong. Thus we read of "tendentious struggles" and "tendentious battles" where *strenuous* should have been placed instead.

Whether correctly or incorrectly, people haven't been using *tendentious* in English for very long. It only came into being in the mid-1800s from the German *tendenziös*, which came from *tendenz* (tendency). The German word stretches back to the Latin *tendentia*, from the verb *tendo* (I stretch out or reach for), clearly showing the idea of preference rather than struggle. Going back to playwrights—probably the most common tendentious thing they have to face are critics who write what they would call very tendentious reviews. But we're sure the critics would disagree.

tendentious (adj): tending toward a particular point of view (often biased or partisan)

---

theory

"There is extensive literature noting that, rather than just a theory, urban density does in fact produce less greenhouse-gas emissions per person than suburban sprawl."

—*FORBES*

Not to worry, *Forbes*, we won't harp on the fact that it should be "fewer" rather than "less" (see page 109). We will, however, talk about the "just a theory" that's in there. We're not criticizing, since *Forbes* used it much as we would. The problem is, this usage drives scientists insane.

To the nonscientific public, a *theory* means "a guess, a supposition, or speculation that isn't proven." To scientists, that sounds closer to a hypothesis (see page 93). A *theory* to them is "a system of testable ideas that explains something and that is supported by a large body of evidence." Relativity, quantum mechanics, the Big Bang, and evolution are all theories. They've been questioned, there have been attempts to refute them, but, while some details about them may have changed, the major thrusts remain relatively unchanged. So theories are far from guesses; they've survived years of testing. To complicate matters, though, even in science sometimes something is called a theory even when it doesn't have empirical support behind it (like the superstring theory) . . . which makes it more of, yes, a hypothesis.

Going back to the "just a theory" issue, let's let astrophysicist Dave Goldberg weigh in: "The problem with the phrase 'just a theory' is that it implies a real scientific theory is a small thing, and it isn't."

Got it? And if you can't trust an astrophysicist, whom can you trust?

theory (n): technically, a system of testable ideas supported by a large body of evidence

THE LIE/LAY CONFUSION:
WE'RE NOT TAKING IT LYING (NOT LAYING) DOWN!

"Lay Lady Lay"—Song title by singer/songwriter/Nobelist Bob Dylan

"Lay Down Sally"—Song title by singer/songwriter Eric Clapton

If Bob Dylan, who won the Nobel Prize for Literature, uses *lie* incorrectly, who are we to complain? Misusing *lie* (in the sense of lying down or laying something down) is everywhere. It's one of the most common errors people make. Bob should have written Lie, Lady, Lie. It doesn't sound nearly as good, and it might be seen as meaning Dylan wanted the lady to tell a falsehood instead of lying down with him, but it would be correct.

See, we're talking about not one but two verbs—one is *to lie*, the other is *to lay*. To be a little technical, that one verb *to lie* is intransitive, which means it doesn't have an object and doesn't do anything to anyone or anything else. (I lie down.) *To lay* is transitive, which means it does have an object to which the verb is doing something. (I lay down my head.) A transitive verb without an object makes no sense. Take the verb "to hit." You wouldn't just say, "I hit." You hit what? So *lay* needs an object. If Clapton told Sally, "Lay down my guitar," he would have been right. But Sally can't lay down. She can, however, lie down.

So if you're talking about lying down as intransitive, you use these forms: *lie* in the present tense, *lay* in the past tense, *lain* as the past participle (as in "I had lain down in bed") and *lying* as the present participle (as in "She was lying on the bed"). If you're talking about laying something else down, you use these forms: *lay*, *laid*, *laid* (past participle, as in "They had laid the pillow on the bed"), and *laying* (present participle, as in "I am laying the pillow on the bed").

Now for one confusing quirk: The old bedtime rhyme "Now I lay me down to sleep" is correct because it uses "lay" transitively, with an object, myself. It could also be written intransitively as "Now I lie down to sleep." Isn't grammar fun? And that's no lie.

tortuous / torturous

"Tortuous Life of a Chinese Slave"

—HEADLINE OF REVIEW, *SOUTH CHINA MORNING POST*

"Catherine Lim's fourth novel has all the ingredients of an utterly trashy read," says the *South China Morning Post* book reviewer. She nevertheless goes on to admire the author's "deft" account of the beatings, the misery of the Chinese slave's "tortuous life."

But *tortuous* doesn't mean "full of torture," it means "twisty," as in "a tortuous road up a mountain." Thinking *tortuous* refers to torture instead is very common; it certainly looks like it should. But here's an etymological twist—*tortuous* comes via the Old French, from the Latin *tortus* (twisting), which comes from the Latin verb *torquere* (to twist).

And now for a little dollop of yet more tortuous etymological confusion: *Torture* and its adjective *torturous*—with an added *r* between the *o* and the *us*—also ultimately derive from the same Latin word, *tortus* (twisting). Think about it: twisting an unwilling body is obviously a pretty torturous thing to endure.

Another less common tortuous mistake (except among lawyers and paralegals) is to confuse *tortuous* and *tortious*. *Tortious* is a legal term meaning "of or relating to a tort" (which is a wrongful act or an infringement upon one's contractual rights). And where do *tort* and *tortious* come from? You guessed it—the old Latin word *torquere* again, in this case, the neuter past participle *tortum* (twisted, distorted). Interestingly, reading complex legal opinions can be both torturous and tortuous but not tortious.

tortuous (adj): twisting and turning
torturous (adj): being tortured

tough road to hoe / tough row to hoe

"The Senator—who's retiring this year—admits it's a tough road to hoe for any conservative to get love from members of the Academy."

—TMZ

Ask yourself: Can a road ever be *easy* to hoe? Why bother saying a specific road is metaphorically tough to hoe if all roads are and no one ever did or does hoe them?

To make sense, the phrase obviously should be "a tough *row* to hoe," which is the original idiom that comes, naturally enough, from farming. In a cornfield, there are many rows, and some can be much harder to hoe than others. Ask any early-American farmer. In fact, tough row hoeing as a metaphorical concept is all-American. It dates back to the pioneering days in the 1800s: Davy Crockett used it in his memoirs in 1835, and it's in many other early books on pioneer life as well. (Although interestingly "hard row to hoe" was used more often than "tough row to hoe.")

As for "road" versus "row" substitutions, the problem with idioms is we really don't think about the meaning of the individual words. Because roads are more common than rows in today's urbanized world, people commonly (and wrongly) replace *row* with *road*. (This kind of substitution is called an "eggcorn," for "acorn," and we meet it all the time in phrases like "dull as dishwater" with "dishwater" substituting for "ditchwater.")

Alas, we have many tough roads to hoe today, especially in sports writing, but also in music (Ghost Town Blues Band's

Hard Road to Hoe). And astonishingly, it shows up even in agricultural writing where you'd think they'd understand but noooooo: "Farming can be a tough road to hoe for the young."

tough row to hoe (phrase): metaphorically, something difficult to do

---

tow the line / toe the line

"But it is a step in the right direction and brands such as Saint Laurent who have promoted the 'heroin chic' look with skeletal models will be the first to have to tow the line."

—HUFFINGTON POST

We are now picturing very tall, extremely thin models tugging on a rope . . . which we suspect is not the right image. The models (and the company) should be *toeing* the line—that is, in this case, obeying the rules—not towing it.

There are different origin stories for the phrase, but they all involve toes. Some sources say the phrase came from runners putting their toes on their marks before a race. In the past, rather than saying "On your mark!" race officials would yell, "Toe the line!" Others say it came from boxing, when boxers stood on either side of a line in the center of the ring before a fight. Still others say it doesn't have anything to do with sports at all, but with the British Navy. In the nineteenth century, seamen would line up on the deck for either inspection or group punishment, their bare feet touching the seams in the wooden deck.

Whichever story is right, one thing is clear: there is no pulling, hauling, lugging, or dragging involved. But that isn't stopping the inexorable rise of *towing*. A look at the Google Ngram Viewer shows the correct "toe the line" is much more used than "tow the line"; but the trend lines also show that "toe the line" is headed down while "tow" is on an upswing. And that's, um, toe bad.

toe the line (phrase): conforming to a set of edicts, accepting the authority of a person or group, or lining up for a race

---

travesty / tragedy

". . . there's a dash of Dickens' *Oliver Twist* and Shakespeare's *Hamlet* too (a good travesty tries to get everyone involved)."
—BUFFALO [NY] NEWS

Many people seem to think that a "travesty" is a "tragedy" . . . which is a tragedy in and of itself.

Okay, perhaps we overstate. But a travesty isn't a tragedy at all. It is "a mockery, a grotesque caricature"—thus the phrase *travesty of justice*, meaning "a mockery of justice." But somewhere along the line, people started using *travesty* to mean *tragedy*, which is why we see politicians bemoaning the travesty ensuing when a bill they didn't want passed passes and the like.

If you know *travesty*'s history, the mockery angle makes a great deal of sense. When *travesty* first appeared in the 1660s, it actually referred to being dressed in a disguise that was ridiculous. It evolved from the French *travesti* (dressed in disguise), from the Italian *travestire* (to disguise), from its original root, the Latin prefix *trans-* (beyond) and *vestire* (to clothe). It first became known to English speakers in 1648 when a satirical work by French poet Paul Scarron included it in its title—*le Virgile travesti en vers burlesques* (Virgil travestied in burlesque verses), and entered the English language meaning just what it means (or is supposed to mean) today: "a grotesquerie, something laughably ridiculous."

Here is an example we found of *travesty* used correctly, if a bit tortuously (see page 180): "The joke of the travesty or the travesty of the joke comment upon both joke and meta-commentary—an inward spiral spiralling outwardly."

travesty (n): a mockery, a groteseque caricature
tragedy (n): event causing great pain or sorrow, a calamity

---

trooper / trouper

"While she continued to sing like a trooper, we're afraid the poncho didn't do much as far as keeping her dry was concerned."

—E! ONLINE

If E! Online wanted to make us think of singer Adele as acting like a police officer or soldier, they succeeded. However, we suspect (actually we're sure of it) that they meant to present Adele as a prime example of a "show must go on!" kind of person. That means they should have used *trouper*, not *trooper*. You can, as the saying goes, swear like a trooper, but you carry on like a *trouper*.

So when to *-oo* and when to *-ou*? It's pretty straightforward, even if it's commonly mistaken. Both words come from the same root—the French *troupe*, which carries the same meaning as its modern version. But today's "trouper" is, logically, part of a troupe—a group of people, usually a theater group, while a "trooper" is a soldier or a police officer. Nowadays, colloquially, when you call someone a "trouper" (spelled correctly), you are saying that person handles hardships or difficulties without complaining, much like an actor on the burlesque circuit who had to keep going from town to town and show to show. When you call them a "trooper," you are talking about someone brave or stalwart, clearly a different meaning, even though some dictionaries now list it as a synonym of *trouper*. But to purists, that is simply not right and could cause them to swear like, yes, troopers.

trooper (n): an entry-level soldier or a police officer
trouper (n): a person belonging to a group, usually of performers

---

unexceptionable / unexceptional

"Furthermore, accounts of voice hearing have been documented throughout human history: recounted by a wide array of pioneers, geniuses, rebels, and innovators that span across the centuries—and also by normal, unexceptionable people like myself.

—HUFFINGTON POST

As you would expect from a word consisting of the prefix *un-* (not) and the adjective *exceptionable*, *unexceptionable* means (drumroll) "not exceptionable." No surprise there.

Yet many people think it is a slightly longer way of saying *unexceptional*. This is, unexceptionably, a mistake.

Something *unexceptionable* is not open to objection, you can't take exception to it. It is fine as it is. Something *unexceptional* is commonplace, more of the same old, same old—as in "the food at this restaurant is unexceptional, so I'm going to give them a mediocre Yelp."

The first recorded use of *unexceptionable* was 1660 historical romance *Bentivolio and Urania*: "All which I have said was done in the Presence of unexceptionable Witnesses." *Unexceptional* was used about a hundred years later, with the *OED* citing its first recorded use in 1775, in British novelist Fanny Burney's early journals: "She bears an unexceptional character." But in this case, *unexceptional* actually means . . . "unexceptionable" (as in the first old definition of *unexceptional*)!

Confused? So were we. But that was then, this is now, and all of the major American dictionaries and grammatists are unanimous: *unexceptional* and *unexceptionable* are unexceptionably different, even though people persist in mixing up the two, particularly in reviews where one can read about such untasty treats as the "unexceptionable tacos" at a new Mexican place . . . which, of course, means that you can't object to the tacos? Waiter, check please!

unexceptionable (adj): not open to objection
unexceptional (adj): ordinary, run-of-the-mill

unique

"Meet One of the Most Unique Homes in Washington DC"
—HEADLINE, *WASHINGTON POST* MAGAZINE

Can there be more than one unique thing? When asked this question, famed author Isaac Asimov said, "No, I am a slight perfectionist in this respect. [Joke]."

Of course, there can't be more than one unique thing. But let's go one further . . . in fact, let's go two further . . . to two authoritative dictionaries. The *OED*'s first, firm definition of *unique* is "of which there is only one." *Merriam-Webster's* is a bit more inclusive. Its third definition of *unique* is "highly unusual, extraordinary, rare, etc.," although it notes that this "common usage is still objected to by some."

Include us in the ranks of the "some," though not as emphatically so as the venerable *New York Times* book reviewer in 1984 who said that such usage was an "indefensible outrage!" Times have changed since then and so has the *Times*—indeed we found a "most unique" in their June 17, 2013, issue. *Unique* in the sense of "rare" is certainly gaining at least grudging acceptance.

But why not have a unique word that means "only one"? For things plural that we might wish to call unique, we can instead say "unusual, very rare, exceptional." We can keep a strong, independent, unique adjective standing proudly alone.

Alas, it's probably a losing battle. During a recent Google search, we found 772,000 entries for "one of the most unique restaurants," along with hundreds of thousands of other not-so-unique uniques. Maybe we'll start saying "one-of-a-kind" instead. Then again, there'll probably soon be ads for "one of the most one-of-a-kind restaurants ever!"

unique (adj): one of a kind

untenable

"How does a woman who had the strength to end what she believes is an untenable marriage steel herself for a reunion that has been promoted and anticipated around the world for months?"

—*DAILY TELEGRAPH* [SYDNEY, AUSTRALIA]

Is marriage an unbearable misery? Maybe so, depending on the marriage, although we certainly hope not. Is it an "untenable" misery? No, never. It can't be. This definition of marriage is untenable. (Well, at least partially untenable.)

Untenable literally means "not capable of being defended." It came from the French *un* (not) and *tenable* (to be held), from the Latin *tenere* (to hold)—and was frequently used in this literal sense, as in this from a British army officer in 1671: "In a council of war the Town was judged untenable." But *untenable* quickly escaped from untenable towns and indefensible military forts and went into other linguistic areas. It now also can mean "insupportable, not able to be coped with," as in an untenable position at work.

But for some reason *untenable* is still not generally accepted in the purely emotional sense. An untenable opinion? Fine. An untenable job? Yup. But an untenable sorrow? Untenable misery? No! say most linguistic purists quite emphatically. (A *Free Dictionary* panel found only 19 percent approved of *untenable* used with emotions.) So, unless you want angry *Free Dictionary* panelists attacking your untenable metaphoric internal linguistic fortress, stick with *unbearable* instead when you want to describe your terrible sorrows or someone's terrible marriage. Or wait a hundred years or so for the language to change. But that would be untenably . . . no, wait, unbearably long.

untenable (adj): not capable of being defended, insupportable

---

utilize

"The Bills conducted their first three summer training camps (1960–62) in East Aurora, NY (about 25 miles south of Buffalo). They utilized the historic Roycroft Inn as their headquarters for housing and food service and the polo fields at the famous Knox Family Estate for practice."

—BUFFALO BILLS WEBSITE

Substitute "used" for "utilized" here and see if there's a difference. The only difference we can see is that *utilized* is longer and sounds needlessly pretentious or clunky. In fact, *utilize* was not much used until the twentieth century. Back in 1942, famous lexicographer Eric Partridge said "utilize is 99 times out of 100, much inferior to use; the other one time it is merely inferior."

That's going a bit too far in our opinion; let's give it a 2 percent approval rating. Fowler's *A Dictionary of Modern English Usage* notes that especially in the past, *utilize* could be distinguished from *use* in the sense that it could mean "to be made good use of, especially of something that was not intended for the purpose but will serve," as in "She utilized her dead laptop as a doorstop."

But is there really much difference if we use *use* instead? Another distinctive variant meaning occurs most often in scientific writing—"to convert to use." Here *utilize* sounds better, and it seems more precise, as in "The body utilizes carbohydrates in fatty acid synthesis." But even here, *use* can be used as well, although it sounds a lot less scientific, for some reason.

In general, *utilize* is just a fancy way of saying *use*, is very overused in academia and business mostly because it sounds more "official," and is usually best not ~~utilized~~ used at all.

utilize (v): to use

---

venal / venial

"The South, in particular, felt that its pastoral society with its ruling elite and slavery-bound servants more closely matched the ideal of ancient Rome than the industrialized society of the North with its venial politicians."

—*THE GREENWOOD ENCYCLOPEDIA OF DAILY LIFE IN AMERICA*

It's a venial sin to use *venial* instead of *venal*.

Well, not really, but note that *venial* is an adjective meaning "slight or forgivable offenses." It *never* refers to people. Not even politicians. So we forgive you if you've committed this venial offense against English. *Venial* is most often seen in Christian theology as an adjective modifying *sin*. A venial sin is one that's pardonable; commit a venial sin or two and you're not on the straight road to hell. (A mortal sin is another matter.) *Greenwood Encyclopedia* should have used the adjective *venal* to describe its politicians, that is, "corrupt, easily bribed." What a difference an *i* makes.

Venial and *venal* come from two different Latin root words. *Venal* comes from *venalis* (put up for sale). It has been traced far back to an early Proto-Indo-European (PIE) prefix *wes-* (to buy or sell), which quickly took on a bad sense—a willingness to sell one's services for sordid motives. One can easily surmise that politicians were bought as far back as prehistory.

Venial, on the other hand, came to English via the Old French word *venial* (pardonable), from Latin *venia*, which scholars suggest is traceable back to another PIE prefix *wen-* (to strive for). This root is found in such words as *venerate*, *venison*, *venery* (the pursuit of sexual pleasure, also hunting), and Venus, the goddess of love. We can easily imagine venal politicians of the past (and present) committing venial sins of venery.

venal (adj): corrupt, easily bribed
venial (adj): pardonable (usually describing sin)

---

verbal / oral

"There has been a recent change at our hospital on how we handle verbal orders. If the Physician is on the unit giving you verbal orders, you are to hand them an order sheet and ask them to write them."

— ALLNURSES.COM

We certainly hope that doctors give verbal orders. Otherwise, they'd be drawing pictures to explain to the nurses what to do, which might be a little confusing. Yes, if you're like the nurses at allnurses.com and most of the rest of us, you probably think that *verbal* specifically means words that are spoken, oral words. But *verbal* simply means "using or pertaining to words" . . . in any manner whatsoever. What the nurses should be talking about are the doctor's oral, or spoken, orders.

Verbal comes via the Latin word *verbalis* (consisting of or pertaining to words; *verbum* means "word"). Hard to argue with that derivation.

But almost everyone ignores it. It's one of the most common mistakes in English, according to the *Daily Telegraph*. The *OED* has examples dating back to 1617 ("The Chamber of the Pallace where verball appeales are decided"). Most dictionaries even allow this usage, albeit as a later definition. But we agree with Bryan Garner (of *Garner's Modern English Usage* and website LawProse) who thinks we should keep a stern distinction between *verbal* and *oral*. Garner mentions that some people may prefer not to use *oral* in this context because of its association with oral sex. His answer: "If you think of 'oral' in a narrow sexual sense, you should immediately wash your mouth out with soap. Otherwise, we may be in danger of losing a perfectly good word." So let's keep our mouths and minds clean and use *verbal* correctly. And instead of saying "oral," we can always say "spoken."

verbal (adj): using or pertaining to words
oral (adj): spoken

verbiage

"The shirt has a large red X across it and verbiage in the picture that read, 'This product has no affiliation to the Notorious B.I.G. estate.'"

—POPCULTURE.COM

Short, sweet, and to the point. So we will be, too: *Verbiage* isn't just words, it's an *excess* of words, which "This product has no affiliation to the Notorious B.I.G. estate" isn't.

This specific meaning is clear when you look at its development. The word entered English in the eighteenth century, from the seventeeth-century French noun *verbiage* (wordiness), from the French verb *verbier* (to chatter), which stemmed from the Latin *verbum* (word). So from the beginning, the emphasis was squarely on the concept of too many words, an overabundance, not just words themselves.

But many people don't appear to know this and instead use *verbiage* as a somewhat longwinded, highfalutin way of saying "words." And . . . they're not completely wrong, depending on whom you consult. *Merriam-Webster's* lists "the way in which something is expressed; wording or diction" as a secondary definition, an addition they made in their 1963 *Seventh Collegiate Dictionary*. Needless to say, many grammar purists take exception to this.

Interestingly, though, it turns out that this isn't just a modern usage at all. The *OED* cites an example from 1804 by none other than the Duke of Wellington in his dispatches: "All that is nothing; the previous verbiage [of the treaty] is thought sufficient to bind us."

So how to verbalize *verbiage*? Because the usual sense is somewhat pejorative (see page 138), conjuring up thoughts of a bombardment of words, we recommend avoiding it.

verbiage (n): too many words

---

wet your appetite / whet your appetite

"To wet their appetite the singer-songwriter released the visuals for his single 'Animal' which not only leaves little to the imagination, but you may lose your virginity for a second time after watching it."

—VIBE

If you talk about wetting your appetite, you're, um, "whrong." You can dampen your appetite or wet your whistle, but those are other things entirely. The word should be *whet*, not *wet*.

Whet means "to sharpen" and always has, dating back to its first appearance in 897 in King Alfred's *Pastoral Care*. It came from the Old English *hwettan* (sharpen, literally; encourage, figuratively) from the German *wetzen* and the Old Germanic χ*watjan*. When you whet your appetite, you are sharpening it, stimulating your desire for something—a very different thing from wetting it. "Whetting one's appetite" as a phrase isn't quite as old, but has been around quite a while, appearing in a 1612 Thomas Dekker play: "[He] seekes new wayes to whet dull appetite." Over time, its usage spread to covering things other than food.

Also over time, "wet your appetite" became more and more common. Some language experts speculate that this came about because it was similar to the older phrase "wet your whistle," to wet your throat, i.e., take a drink, which, as the *OED* notes, first appeared in 1386, in the Towneley Mysteries ("Had She oones Wett Hyr Whystyll She couth Syng full clere Hyr pater noster") But to complicate matters, the *OED* notes that *wet* and *whet* were even confused in this phrase, with the incorrect "whet your whistle" emerging back in the late 1600s.

Just because it's old doesn't mean it's okay, though. Use *whet* . . . unless you want to drive us to drink.

whet your appetite (phrase): stimulate desire for something